Kema's Journey is a true story. Only the names of the kennel owners and their location have been changed to protect their identities.

Copyright © 2018 by Kenneth R. Luchterhand
All rights reserved. This book or any portion thereof may not be reproduced or used in any manner whatsoever without the expressed written permission of the author except for the use of brief quotations in a book review.

Printed in the United States of America

First Printing, September 2018
Second Printing, Black and White version, March 2021

Kenneth R. Luchterhand
ISBN-13: 978-1-7365891-0-6

BISAC: Pets / Dogs / General

Prologue

I was telling my tale about how we got Kema to a group of people and the living conditions we found her in. I was being very descriptive and assumed everyone was connecting with me until I got a question from one of the women that floored me.

She asked me, "What do you like about dogs? I mean, I'm not a dog person, so I don't know why people like dogs so much."

I was dumbfounded. I didn't answer right away because I couldn't. My mind couldn't figure out how to answer a question like that. There weren't any words that would suffice.

It's kind of like someone asking, "Why do you love your mother," or the question "Tell me what's it like to see" coming from a blind person. I've never had to ponder why I like – no, love – dogs. It just comes from within and never needed an explanation.

I could have said something like the fact that dogs love you unconditionally, but that's not all of it. I could have said that I like the fact that dogs only want to please me, so they will do anything for me. I could have said that dogs are extremely intelligent and easy to train because they understand so much. Or I could have said that dogs are so warm and fluffy and loving.

But I didn't. Instead, I thought and said the first thing that came to mind.

"That's a difficult one to answer," I said. "I have had dogs all my life. I can't imagine life without them. But I guess what I like about them is that the dogs I've had have bonded with me so that we live together and do everything together and are best friends."

I gave an example of Thorn, my previous Gordon setter, who lived with me in Stevens Point, Wisconsin, while I worked at the Stevens Point Journal newspaper. I could come home at noon and spend time with him, then go back to work. After work, and on weekends, he and I would go out on adventures. We'd go on walking trails through woods, to the lake, and especially along the walking trail beside the Wisconsin River. In fact, most of the time I would ride my bicycle and he'd pull me with the leash. When we came to a stop sign, I'd clamp on the brakes and yell for him to stop. He had so much energy that he would often keep pulling, and my brakes would be creating a cloud of smoke as I tried to convince him to give it a rest.

On summer evenings, we'd walk to the local ice cream stand where I would get a cone and he'd get a "puppy cup" and eat them side-by-side each other.

He'd sleep on my bed. He would sit beside me on the couch while I watched television. And when we went anywhere, he'd be the first one into the car.

That wasn't the best answer I could have given, but I was hoping to paint a picture for her just why dogs are so important to me.

"So, dogs are a substitute for humans for you?" she asked.

No. Not at all. Two different things altogether. But I didn't have an answer because, obviously, she just didn't understand the connection and bond that we had formed. I realized that a lot of people don't understand because, to them, dogs are just animals and somehow lesser life forms than humans. Perhaps they grew up never having a dog in their lives.

But I know dog people do understand. It's more about who you are and how you love rather than some rational explanation. The love for dogs just can't be put into words. It's more of a feeling.

KEMA'S Journey

By Ken Luchterhand

Chapter One: The Search

Something in me told me it was time for another dog.

There was nothing wrong with the one I had, mind you, but somehow I got the itch for another dog. I wanted a Gordon setter, like the one I had before I got our English setter, Buddy.

That Gordon setter, Thorn, was the smartest dog I ever had. I could write an entire book about his personality and adventures. He died of cancer in 2006, 10 years earlier. I was missing him.

I think the main reason I got "more dogs" on the brain is that I attended a dog show in January 2016, following a young woman who is an avid dog show fanatic. I was writing an article for the newspaper about her passion and all of what goes into the effort of showing dogs. I learned that she had several dogs and I was amazed at how she could have that level of energy.

I also admired the setters at the show, looking jealously at all the beautiful loving woofers and I ended up wanting another to run, jump and play with. We had Buddy, but he was 10 years old at the time and slowing down considerably. There is nothing wrong with having an older dog, but I was missing the quirky behavior of a Gordon setter.

Gordon setters are one of four recognized setter breeds, the others being the Irish, English, and the Red and White Irish setter. While similar in size and body structure, I found that Gordons had by far the most personality. They will make a person laugh one moment and be totally amazed at their intelligence in the next moment. They are medium-sized, not extremely big or small, and weigh about 50 to 60 pounds. They are black with the usual brown markings on the muzzle, eyebrows, and lower legs, the same as Dobermans, Rottweilers, some dachshunds, and raccoon-hunting "coon" dogs.

After talking to other Gordon setter owners, I soon learned that Gordons share some particular habits and behaviors that seem unique to the breed.

Gordons are not common, therefore many people seeing a Gordon for the first time will not recognize the breed. In fact, they are so uncommon that I have difficulty finding the usual doggie merchandise featuring any setters, but especially Gordons. I can't find calendars, mugs, tee shirts, or anything with a Gordon.

I knew my search for the elusive Gordon would not be easy.

I began looking for a Gordon setter online, the easiest method since I sit on the computer all day at work and have unlimited use of the Internet. I found a woman who was selling pups near the Twin Cities, but after several correspondences, I learned I had to make my mind up quickly, something an old man like me can't do. I don't do anything quickly these days.

I would get really poor quality pictures of the pups from her and soon there were only two males left. The size difference between the two was striking. I was convinced the smaller pup was the runt of the litter, so I chose the bigger one. Besides, the bigger one had light tan markings while the smaller one had very dark tan markings, almost to the point of being all black.

I let the breeder know which one I preferred and soon got a reply that the bigger one was spoken for. I was still undecided, and the fact that I was deciding on a pup that was rejected by every other adoptee had me puzzled.

I'm probably one of the least impulsive people in the world and very cautious. It takes me forever to make a decision that would affect me on a long-term basis.

The woman gave me until the weekend to decide on him. I was thinking that I don't like making sight-unseen and hasty decisions, something I would have to live with for at least the next 10 years. I said no, that I would keep looking for the right one at the right time.

So, my search continued.

I was commenting on Facebook on one of the Gordon setter pages that I often see pups available for sale in Europe, but seldom see any in the United States. Now that I have better connections, I have found it easier to find a Gordon setter puppy. I got a comment back from a Gordon owner in southeastern Illinois, telling about a woman, Alice, in Kentucky who had a pregnant female due to having pups soon. She gave me a phone number and I called.

Alice said she did have a pregnant female and the pups were due any day. She would put my name on the list and I was number four, she told me. So I waited.

About a week went by and I was informed that 11 pups were born. I was extremely happy and I could hardly contain my excitement.

A few more days passed and I received an email telling me that a tragedy had happened. Apparently, the mother had killed all the puppies. It was her first litter.

I was devastated. I assumed that I would begin searching again. I found some breeders in Wisconsin; however, the litters wouldn't arrive until summer and would not be ready for adoption until about September. Ugh.

Alice sent me a follow-up email saying how disgusted she was that her female killed all the pups. She said, "I have no place in my kennel for her." She asked if I wanted her, and said that she would make me a good deal on her. I wasn't sure what that meant, but I was eager to hear the offer. Regardless of cost, I was interested.

For a long time, I was on the fence. I really wanted a puppy, but I also considered that a puppy was more destructive and took a lot more training than an adult dog. Just the physical dimensions of a full-size dog versus a puppy enabled one to do certain things better than the other. I sent Alice an email asking for some photos of the dog. She sent a few, although they weren't the best quality. Kema looked awkward, as though she was being restrained for the photos.

I thought about it for a while and talked it over extensively with my wife, Joanna. She heard my story and looked at the photos of Kema, then told me we should go down to get her. I called Alice to let her know we were coming to get her.

At first, I mispronounced Kema's name when talking to Alice. I had never encountered such a name, so I thought maybe it was pronounced "Kemma," but I was corrected by Alice that it was a long "e" and pronounced "Keeema." I never did ask her how Kema got her name.

I looked at the calendar and I figured out that I had off the day after Easter and our son, Kennan, had off from school and Joanna had two days off her work after Easter. The best option was to go during the Easter holiday, we agreed, so I told Alice we would be coming then.

The next step was to go get her, which was a haul. Google maps said the fastest route was about 10 hours. Although I wasn't looking forward to a trip to Kentucky, I was anxious to meet the dog waiting for me at the end of my journey.

Chapter Two: Heading South

I made hotel reservations by the internet for Elizabethtown, Kentucky, and Joanna, Kennan, Buddy, and I started out early Saturday morning, the day before Easter. We loaded my wife's SUV, a 2006 Mitsubishi Endeavor, and made fairly good time; but we stopped twice to eat, thereby expending two hours more. When we got between Indianapolis and Louisville, traffic came to a halt. I mean shut-off-the-engine-and-walk-around standstill - bumper to bumper as far as the eye can see. A helicopter flew overhead to presumably extricate an accident victim, and three wreckers came flying by on the shoulder of the road. We were sitting there for an hour and a half.

The daylight was gone when we started moving again. The Interstate took us through what looked like downtown Louisville, which was a nerve-racking experience. We eventually got beyond that and arrived at the hotel in Elizabethtown at about 10:30 pm, which equated to a 13-hour trip. We felt beaten.

I expected to receive some fuss from the hotel staff when it came to having Buddy in our hotel room. However, they didn't seem concerned at all. In fact, many people would make some kind of adoring comment when we were walking through the lobby with him, either heading for the room or to do his business outside on their lawn.

The next day, I made a phone call to Alice and told her we would like to see the female dog she was offering us. She gave us directions, about a 30-mile drive to the west, but told us the drive to their farm was a little tricky. We should go to the Johnson General Store and then give her a call. Her husband or daughter would meet us there, she said.

We drove through the winding Kentucky countryside, observing farms placed equidistant from each other and noticing that no crops were grown. Every farm was pasture only and held mostly sheep and horses, but very few cattle. Everything was green, something we had not seen yet in Wisconsin because the weather was still toying with winter back home.

We arrived at the Johnson General Store and took a peek inside, after calling to let Alice know we had arrived. The merchant was a throwback in time, a memory from my childhood when general stores had everything, even a front porch. I chuckled as I walked down the aisles and saw that just about any type of necessity was for sale: food, clothing, hardware, medicines, and farm supplies. The funniest part was the wooden sign hanging from the ceiling at the back of the store. It said "Outhouses" and had an arrow beneath, pointing to the right. I believed there were outhouses outside, through that door, but I never actually went to check them out.

I went back outside the store to walk Buddy around and to watch for a car, or truck, or buggy. Joanna and Kennan were inside, buying stuff, and then they joined me to wait for the arrival of Alice or her husband or daughter.

Soon a car came rolling up from our left, pulled into one of the parking spaces, a young woman at the wheel, and the driver's side window motored down.

"Dough-gies?" she asked loudly. She didn't say "doggies," otherwise I would have understood her. But instead, it was a twang that sounded like "dough – gies."

I said, "What?"

"Are you the dough-gie people?"

"Umm. Yeah," I said.

We approached her window.

"That's quite an accent you have," I said.

"That's what happens when you come back here," she said. I didn't ask where she'd been. I wasn't sure if she meant coming back to the general store or Kentucky.

We agreed that I would follow her, so she whipped the car around and we followed with our vehicle for a few miles, then turned right onto a narrow, twisty road. A few more miles later, we turned down a long driveway, with a house on the right and a barn on the left. We parked by the other vehicles on the right and were immediately greeted by a chorus of dogs in kennels on the end of the small barn.

The noise was deafening, and as I walked around the end of the kennels, I wasn't impressed. It looked dirty and most runs had two dogs in them. The young woman, the one we had followed to the place, ran into the house and soon an older woman, whom I assumed to be Alice, began slowly walking our way.

She was a short woman, with dark hair; rather stocky, and wearing slippers. Yeah, I couldn't stop staring at those slippers. She stepped around puddles of something, which I was hoping was water but was thinking it was pee from the kennels, and then proceeded to step around dog poop. I'm not sure she missed them all; in fact, I'm pretty certain she didn't.

James, her husband, came around the corner and introduced himself. I was hoping to see the stereotypical hillbilly while in Kentucky, and I was rather happy I finally met one. James was just as I had pictured a hillbilly to look. He was tall and slender, wore bib overalls, had a wrinkly face and a long gray beard, and walked a little hunched over.

He reached up with one hand to shake mine. I noticed a fresh wound on his hand as he brought it up to mine, with blood still evident, but the wound never touched my hand, so I wasn't too worried. I quickly looked to his other hand to see if he had one of those moonshine jugs in it but, alas, it was not to be. Darn.

I could see the entrance to the kennel was locked with a padlock. James went to an abandoned pickup truck, parked just outside the kennel, opened a door, and grabbed a key from the glove compartment. He sauntered over and unlocked the gate, then went inside the chain-link fence enclosure, at the front of the approximate 10 individual kennel runs, which were side-by-side. The dog barking, which began when we drove up, now hit a high point, making it difficult for any conversation to take place. The cracked concrete had a scattering of dog turds, and trickles of urine coursed from several of the runs into a myriad of pathways.

We were introduced to Kema, a skinny young Gordon setter who came to the front gate of her run in curiosity, but cowered when anyone approached. She had a cute face, but her bones were clearly visible beneath her black and tan coat. The hair on her rear legs was wet. I didn't even want to know with what. She was smaller than any Gordon I had ever seen.

"Wow," I thought to myself. I didn't know what to say to Alice and James. She retreated every time I approached the chain-link fence.

"She's smaller than what I expected," I finally said.

"Yes, she is. I think the Gordon setters in France are smaller," she said, referring to her lineage. Previously she had alluded to a claim that Kema was a descendant of a Grand Champion in France. However, that was back when we were talking about me getting one of her puppies.

I walked down the line, looking at the dogs in each of the kennel runs. I noticed that all were at the front, wagging tails, barking, and wanting attention. That is, all but Kema.

She would come to the front and bark but retreat every time anyone came near. My heart was sinking because this was not the dog I had pictured in my mind, but also I felt deeply sorry. Somehow I wanted to make her trust me and to give her a better life.

"Why don't you go in there and sit for a while to see if she warms up to you?" Alice suggested.

I opened the kennel door and stepped inside, with Kema going toward the back and curling up on a sort of bed, but it was really small and had no bottom padding. It was more or less some cloth between her and the concrete floor. I went to pet her awhile and then she got up and went to the side of her run where she muzzled, the best she could through the woven wire wall, with two English setters on the other side, barking occasionally. Kema sat down, leaning against the fence.

It seemed as though she were seeking security from the other two dogs. Perhaps she had bonded with them and they were good friends. Now, with me making her feel uneasy, she needed some emotional support from her closest friends, who were now just on the other side of the wire.

I squatted next to her, talking gently and stroking her

head, occasionally lifting one of her long floppy ears.

"Don't be afraid, girl. I'm not going to hurt you. I'm your friend," I said to her. Her head pointed away, with her looking at me out of the corners of her eyes, wanting to believe in me, but somehow not able to let go of her fear.

After a time of talking and petting at arm's length, I finally gave up, partly because I'm not sure I was accomplishing anything and partly because I couldn't sit in a squatting position for long before I started to hurt. I exited the pen and rejoined Alice and Joanna. I wasn't sure where Kennan was, but I figured he went back to the Endeavor to be with Buddy.

"She's nice," I said, not knowing what else to say. The statement was true but didn't tell the full story. Meanwhile, Joanna went into the kennel to be with her and she was having little luck trying to get Kema to warm up to her.

Alice and I stood by the back fence, watching Joanna and making small talk. Alice asked what is my occupation and she told me that she had been a journalist, too, but had to give it up because of her health. We touched on other subjects, other than talk about Kema. My mind was still trying to sort through it all.

She explained that a friend convinced her to begin breeding dogs as a business and that she could make some decent money in the process. That shocked me and I was afraid to ask her questions. I wondered how wonderful animals such as dogs could be treated this way as a means to make a profit.

At one point, she turned slightly to her right and pointed at a round wire corncrib.

"Those dogs are in jail," she said. "They keep on escaping, so we have to keep them in there."

I was astounded by what she said. Those dogs truly were in jail. It reminded me of the movies where a prisoner attempts to escape but gets caught and placed in the "hot box" for punishment. I felt so sorry for those doggies, I just wanted to run over and release them. I wondered if I had stumbled upon something similar to a World War II prisoner of war camp, where all the occupants wanted nothing more than to escape their living hell and were willing to risk death to do it.

Alice asked what I thought and if I wanted Kema. I hated to commit to anything, my mind still reeling. I wanted to take Kema and run, but I also didn't know if I could allow the other dogs to stay behind in these conditions. My mind was trying to comprehend all that I was seeing and attempting to understand – I wasn't sure of everything that was happening here. I had to rethink this whole thing, not just about Kema, but this shock to my conscience. I knew I had to get Kema out, but I wasn't sure what else I could have done. At home, it would have been easy to make a complaint, but here I was a foreigner. I liked James and Alice. They might have started out with good intentions, but it was obvious that they weren't able to keep up with the demands of running a kennel. As a result, the dogs were the ones who were paying the price.

"We'd like to see a few of the tourist spots in Kentucky, like Mammoth Cave. If you don't mind, I would rather not take her right now. But we can spend a day or so in Kentucky and maybe come back on Monday morning," I said.

We came that far, we wanted to make the most of the trip and not immediately turn around and head home right away.

"Sure, Kema's lived here this long, it won't hurt for her to stay a little longer," she said. "You go do your family thing and then let me know."

Before we left, I gave her four blocks of cheese from Wisconsin. As I shut the door and drove down the driveway, I breathed a sigh of exhaustion – not physical, but mental. I didn't know what to think. I needed time.

We drove back to Elizabethtown, trying to decide what to do next. It was about noon and we were thinking maybe it would be too late to go down south to Mammoth Cave. It might be better to plan a whole day for it. Instead, Kennan wanted to go to the stores to look for Halo toys, objects related to a video game, so we headed for the local Walmart and then the shopping mall, which was just across the highway from the Walmart. I stayed with Buddy, either in the Endeavor or walking him around, while Joanna and Kennan spent time shopping.

That evening we ate at a more expensive restaurant, like Ruby Tuesday or something like that, just so we could kick back and relax and have a good meal.

Chapter Three: Exploring the Caves

The next morning was Easter. We felt a little guilty because we didn't go to church or make any type of observation of the religious holiday. It was a little difficult to do anything regarding observing Jesus' resurrection since we were far from home, so we did so in our minds and gave respect and devotion in our hearts.

After some free continental breakfast at the hotel, we set out for Cave City and, from there, Mammoth Cave National Park. The winding route led us to a large visitor center and parking lot. The day was still early, yet the place was bustling with tourists. After parking, we approached the building and I saw a man and woman dressed in National Park uniforms. I asked about the cave tours and they said all guided tours were sold out for the day.

"You have to reserve those in advance. They sell out quickly," the man said. "The only one available is the self-guided tour."

The three of us, plus Buddy, stood in front and wondered what to do next. We had come a long way to be skunked. I decided to go inside and get the tickets for the self-guided tour.

"Can he go inside with me?" I asked at the visitor center building, pointing to Buddy, who stood beside me while I held his leash.

"No. Not unless he is a service dog," he said.

Ugh. Okay, I gave the leash to Joanna and told her to wait for me while I went inside to buy some tickets before all those were gone. I later learned that they never stop selling the self-guided cave tour, no matter how many people show up.

I went inside with Kennan, waited in line a short time, and was directed to one of the many ticket sellers at a long counter. The cost of the tour was $10 each, so I bought one for each of us and was told the cave we were to visit was down a trail that started out the back door of the visitor center.

Kennan and I went back outside, got Joanna and Buddy, and walked around the visitor center to the trail that sloped down to the right from the building. The day was already heating up, something we weren't used to since we still had snow on the ground at home. Pretty soon Buddy's tongue was hanging out of his mouth from the heat.

We reached the site of the cave entrance where there were three park rangers, a metal railing, and an entrance arrangement. We had to wait for enough people so that the park rangers could give us an informative talk about rules and conduct and what we were about to see.

The mouth of the cave was big and we could see many people walking up the concrete steps to leave. They were herded through a gate, similar to a metal detector at an airport, with a chemical mat at their feet. We were told this was to kill all the fungi and viruses that have been causing bats to get sick and die. Supposedly the fungus and viruses still exist in the cave.

I asked a park ranger if Buddy could go with us on the tour. I was told "no." I had to ask, but I wasn't surprised by the answer. After hearing about the disease that exists there, I'm not sure I'd let him go in there anyway.

Joanna and Kennan went into the cave, and I said I would wait with Buddy. One of the park rangers told me there were trails I could explore in the meantime and that it should take about a half-hour for them to conclude their cave explorations. If they came back before me, he said he would tell them to wait for me.

I took Buddy down a steep trail, which eventually wound up beside a green river to our right. Buddy wanted to get down there in the worst way to get a drink. He was panting like crazy. The embankment was muddy and steep. I tried navigating the embankment but found myself sliding down the embankment with no control and no stopping. Somehow, I managed to dig my heels in and climb back to the top, abandoning all hope of getting safely to the river. If we had slid down, we would have plunged into the river with no way to get out.

After a little more exploration, we went back. We were waiting when one of the rangers told me that Joanna and Kennan were looking for us and had gone back to the tourist center. Apparently, the guy who was going to inform them had left for lunch. Buddy's tongue was hanging out and I was concerned that he needed water soon. In the back of my mind, I was thinking about Kema and I was wondering how she dealt with the heat, especially since she couldn't escape it by going into an air-conditioned building.

I found Joanna and Kennan, gave Buddy some water,

left him with them, and then I went on my own cave tour. I wasn't impressed. It looked like just one long tube with no formations or anything. Talking with Joanna and Kema, they said they weren't impressed, either. We went on to get lunch in Cave City, then played a round of miniature golf. We considered going back to the hotel but decided to give the cave thing one last try. There were billboards and advertisements for Diamond Caverns and I had heard it was pretty good, so we headed in that direction. Once there, we found a big gift shop and tours departing every 20 minutes. Someone had to stay with Buddy and Joanna was not feeling up to the rigors of climbing and squeezing through narrow passages and walking on uneven surfaces. She volunteered to stay behind.

This cave was much better, with stalactites, stalagmites, and all the neat things you expect to see in caves. Joanna bought us each a tee shirt and we headed back to the hotel after our adventure.

That night, I could tell Buddy was getting sick of living in the hotel. He didn't want to stay in the room and he only wanted to get back in our vehicle. He was telling us that he wanted to go home. I sympathized with him, as I wanted to go home too.

That night, we were hit with a severe thunderstorm and the power was out for more than an hour. Luckily, we had bought Kennan a battery-powered portable DVD player for the trip. We watched some of that and I dinked around on my smartphone until the electrical power came back on.

Chapter Four: Getting Kema

The next morning, we were anxious to get going. I checked my smartphone and saw that Alice had sent me an email. She was concerned that we hadn't returned and thought that maybe we had changed our minds and headed back home. I didn't respond, partly because I had previously told her our plans and schedule and nothing had really changed, and partly because we were headed there anyway. It didn't pay for me to write back when we'd be there in a few minutes.

We packed our luggage and loaded it into the Endeavor, then headed for James and Alice's place. I told Joanna that I still wasn't absolutely sure that I wanted Kema, but she kept reminding me that we couldn't leave her there, living in those conditions. My conscience wouldn't allow it. In reality, I had made my mind up long ago that we were going to bring her home with us. Perhaps I was testing her to make sure she wanted Kema, too.

We drove to the farm where Kema stayed with my mind wandering all over the place, wondering if she was a permanently ruined dog, if she could ever trust again, or if my heart would melt when I saw her again and she would come willingly into my arms. I somewhat dreaded seeing all those dogs, all of them barking as if to say, "Save me!" I wanted them all out of that situation.

We found the place once again and drove down the driveway. A chorus of barking erupted as we parked in the same place we had before alongside the broad side of the barn. No one was around, so I walked around the truck and along the edge of the chain-link fence at the front of the pad in front of the kennel runs. I was dumbfounded to find a thick mound of dog poop extending along the whole outside edge of the fence. It probably was easier to dump the poop over the fence than to dispose of it properly, I reasoned. I had to walk further away from the fence in order not to step in any poop, but even that task seemed difficult.

I walked along until I saw Kema in her run, looking through her kennel run chain link door. She would come to the front and bark, but then go back along the sides and interact with the other dogs who were also barking. It seemed that she needed their assurance that everything was all right.

"She's coming," Joanna yelled to me. She and Kennan stayed near the vehicles and closer to the entrance of the kennel runs. I walked back to see Alice walking very slowly and carefully, as though she were hurting. I looked to make sure - yep, she was still wearing her house slippers.

"I was thinking you changed your mind," she said as she got closer. "I didn't hear from you, so I thought maybe you weren't coming back for her."

I was wondering why she thought that, since we had told her we were going to visit the caves and other attractions and probably would be back Monday morning. I decided to ignore it and move on.

"No, we came back," I said.

"James will be here in a few minutes. He says his back is troubling him, and I think he fell. But he won't say that," Alice said.

About that time, James came walking toward us just as gingerly as Alice had. I checked to see if he had a moonshine jug in his hand, but no – no such luck.

"Uh oh," I said. "You don't look so good. What's the matter?"

"Oh – my back is acting up," he said. He shuffled over to unlock the chain-link door once again. "I'll bring her out to you."

Disappearing from view for a while, he soon appeared at the main kennel door again, this time with a cowering Kema at his side. He held a frayed, tattered, and ratty leash in his hand, extending down to Kema's neck. He brought her over to me and asked if I had a leash with me. He pointed down to the leash around her neck and showed me that he had looped the end of the leash through the handle so that it essentially choked her when the leash was pulled tight.

"My leash broke, so I had to loop it around her neck," he said.

She had a skinny, frayed nylon collar, so I retrieved a leash from the Endeavor and snapped it onto the "D" ring on her collar. James took his leash off and I stood with her in front of me. I could tell that she had no experience walking on a leash, so I didn't attempt that. I stood there, petting her gently and talking to her while she cowered and looked around nervously.

I was uncertain what to do next because basically, it would have been a struggle to walk with her. Everything that was to be said had been said, so I turned the end of the leash over to Joanna and I proceeded to take out suitcases from the back of the Endeavor and turn the crate 90 degrees so that the opening was pointed to the back.

"Oh good," James said. "You have a crate. I was wondering about that." It was then Buddy raised his head above the back part of the back seat and looked at what I was doing. James said he didn't know we had a dog with us, so he went to the open passenger door to visit with Buddy for a while. I opened the crate door and bent over, not sure how Kema might react to me picking her up.

"Will she bite?" I asked because, from my experience, when dogs are nervous, they sometimes nip out of fear that they're being attacked.

"No, no. She's gentle."

I raised her up and put Kema inside the crate, then latched the door and turned the crate back, placing the baggage inside however I could make it fit. I could hear her turning inside, banging against the inside of the crate.

Reaching inside my back pocket, I took out a bank envelope, the kind that banks give you when you request cash, and counted out six one-hundred-dollar bills.

"Thank you," Alice said. "Well, I guess that's everything. I hope you have good luck with her."

"Uh. Did you have some papers to go with her, like her rabies certificate and her AKC papers?"

"Oh yes," she said. "I almost forgot." Alice walked back to the house and retrieved about four or five papers, one of them with a rabies tag taped to it. "You have to have a rabies tag to cross state lines."

By this time, Buddy was drooling like a garden hose, making everything slobbery and wet in the back seat. That was a characteristic of Buddy. He would drool incessantly whenever he got nervous or around other dogs, besides drooling for food. Kennan was in the back seat with Buddy, complaining because the slobber was getting all over him, the seat, the doors and windows, and anything else he could get drool on.

I thanked Alice and James and we took off down the driveway. We were not even back onto the roadway when it started: the barking. Kema barked and barked and barked. Being in an enclosed space like the inside the Endeavor, the noise was deafening.

"Woof, woof, woof," she said, not liking it a bit. To my

knowledge, she had only ridden in a vehicle once in her life before, and that was to the vet and groomer shortly before we got her. I remember Alice writing to me, saying that Kema was a nervous wreck.

We tried talking to her, singing, playing the radio loud, or whatever we could think of. Nothing stopped her barking. That, along with Buddy's nervous anxiety, made for a ride that would nearly drive us all insane.

"What if she barks all the way home?" I asked Joanna. "I don't think I can handle this."

It would have been worse if not for the fact Joanna kept slipping her doggie treats through the wire mesh in the crate.

We all looked at each other, wondering what to do next. I was hoping for a miracle, something to shut the dog up before our ears ruptured. Also, Kema's smell was ... well, let's just say it was strong. My head began to swim. The odor wasn't just from feces, but a combination of everything gross the mind can imagine, a smell she brought with her from the kennel.

We made it back to Elizabethtown at about 11 am, later than I had hoped. We wanted to get back home in one shot, stopping as few times as possible, and I was getting antsy about the late departure. We grabbed some food to take along from the local gas station and hit the Interstate.

It wasn't long before Kema went silent. I looked at Joanna.

"Did she just die?" I asked. I am sure Joanna didn't know if I was kidding or not. She looked back and saw Kema's head through the wire mesh vent in her crate.

"No, she's okay," she said. What a relief. We decided to enjoy the moment and see how long the silence would last.

Actually, we went a lot farther than I expected with no problems. We all became road-weary and wanted to get home. It seemed like it was taking forever. The goal was to get to Janesville, where I knew a Petco existed. We needed some more dog food and maybe some treats to pacify the dogs for the rest of the trip.

We reached Janesville during rush hour, at about 5 pm and Joanna went inside to buy some dog food while I took Kema for a walk along the grassy edge of a parking lot, hoping she would go potty and take a drink of water. She seemed clumsy and as though she didn't know exactly what to do while on a leash, but she did eventually take a pee. Meanwhile, Kennan was bouncing between the store and me, not helping out anyone in particular.

She was definitely shy and fearful of everything. At one time a car drove by and she flinched and didn't know what to do. I was delighted that, during a calm period, she stood still as I petted her as if she enjoyed finally getting some attention.

Joanna returned with a large bag of dog food, and we packed up to head home once again. I could tell Kema wasn't too happy with the prospect of going back in the crate for another long ride, but the end was near. We only had about two and a half hours more to go.

The drive seemed even longer this time because we were anxious to get home. The closer we got, the longer it seemed because we could sense home up ahead.

We finally arrived home at about 8 pm, which gave us some time to unload and relax before heading for bed. We knew it wasn't going to be easy because we were fearful the new "dough-gie" was going to keep us awake all night.

I realized that adjusting to living in a house instead of a kennel might be a challenge for Kema. After all, she had never been inside one before.

When we arrived home from the long drive from

Kentucky, I was apprehensive as to how Kema might respond to living with humans in a box. The box was built for human habitation, not for dogs, and all the amenities were built for human usage. For instance, all the faucets were made for human hands, not dog paws. The toilet was designed for humans sitting on them, not dogs, and the remotes for televisions and VCRs and DVRs and satellite receivers were for human fingers, not dog toes.

However, some house furnishings could work for either man or dog. They included sofas, recliners, and beds, which we learned could occupy both species at the same time but not very comfortably.

So, when Kema went into the house, she needed to do what all dogs do in new territory: sniff out the place. She quickly walked from room to room, smelled everything she could, and looked at every object everywhere.

In our house, the normal procedure upon entering the house is to turn on the television. Rarely is the television off, even if we are not watching it, so that we have the noise to make everything seem normal.

One of us turned on the television when we had been home for only 10 minutes. The result was something unexpected. Kema looked at the movement from a show, heard the noise, and went crazy. She got angry at the thing, barking as if it was an intruder into our house that needed to be shown who is boss.

After a minute or so of nonstop barking and posturing across the floor, we decided to turn the thing off, at least for now. Some quiet time would be beneficial for all of us.

We unloaded the suitcases and other trip items from the Endeavor and brought them into the house. The suitcases were placed on the bed for unloading, so Joanna began the task while I made another trip to the vehicle. Kema, already having established some type of close relationship, jumped up on the bed to see what she was doing.

I heard another series of "bark, bark, bark." I asked what was going on when I entered the house. Joanna was laughing hysterically while the barking continued. I soon found out that Kema was shocked to see her reflection in a mirror for the first time in her life; therefore, she was certain there was another Gordon setter in the house who needed to be barked at. She was growling and staring into the mirror above Joanna's dresser while standing on the bed. It took a lot to get her to stop.

Once we were settled in and resting in the living room, Kema decided to get comfortable with Joanna on the couch. While sitting on the floor, she shyly put her nose on her lap and then her paws when Joanna started to pet her. After a few minutes of this attention, she jumped onto the couch and leaned on Joanna, pushing her body tightly against her. If the petting stopped, Kema pushed her nose under her hand, as if to say, "Don't stop. I never got this kind of attention before and I don't ever want it to end."

This went on for an hour or so until finally, we had to attempt to get some sleep. The long drive was exhausting and we needed to get our rest.

Chapter Five: Settling In

That first night wasn't as bad as it could have been – but it was bad enough. We put Kema in the crate to sleep, first in the living room, then in our bedroom, in the hopes she would feel comfortable knowing we were near. Every so often during the night, she would startle us with a series of barks. That sort of awakening was a shock to our systems and I hurried so as not to allow her barking to fully awaken everyone in the county. I got her on the leash and promptly took her outside. But to no avail; she never pooped or peed when I was walking her. I think that first night I got up about five times.

We only knew of one time that she pooped and that was in the living room when we weren't looking. From that point on, we never saw her do anything more, inside or out.

During the week, it didn't get much better. Kema would sleep for a while and then start barking and want attention. I'd take her out on the leash and she wouldn't pee or poop, so I'd stumble back into the house and try to go back to sleep, which wasn't easy because the cold air had a way of waking me up. The next few days were difficult for me at work, since sleep deprivation made it difficult to think.

After about four days, we decided to leave her out of the crate at night, since she was becoming accustomed to sleeping on the couch, the recliner, and various places on the floor around the house.

We were hoping she was actually peeing and pooping outside, although we never saw it. I mean, logically, she was eating and that digested food had to go somewhere, but we just weren't sure where. We were hoping she was eliminating when out of sight and that everything was normal.

Meanwhile, Kema developed a great affection for Joanna. She got so excited to see Joanna that her whole back end would wag, not just her tail. And she would jump up on Joanna, planting her front feet on her chest. She liked Kennan, too. She would let him do just about anything to her, including rough play.

But for me, it was completely different. She was timid when she was around me.

Chapter Six: A New Home

Kema was not accustomed to her new surroundings. This I knew. She did not know us – not the new family she just adopted, and not the land she soon would romp upon. The first few weeks after she arrived, whenever she went outside, I was tethered to her via the leash. I had to make certain she didn't make a mad dash for Kentucky and I'd never see her again.

The first three or four nights we had her, she would get restless so I would brave the cold and take her for walks in the darkness. That got old in a hurry. One day I was too tired and too lazy to put on some shoes and go outside with the "dough-gies," so I let Buddy and Kema outside together completely unleashed and untethered. I watched through the window and saw Kema attempting to play with Buddy. She was jumping over his back and boxing him in the face with her paws. I noticed that she was quite skilled in using her paws as hands.

Buddy couldn't keep up with her level of activity, so he eventually went into a defensive mode and retreated under the steps to hide from her. She would do this twirling thing that looked odd. She would spin herself around stiff-legged so that it looked like she would flip 360 degrees without bending her body or flexing a muscle. It was almost too unreal to believe. Of course, I only caught it once on video because it was so unpredictable.

Once outside and on her own, she took the chance to test her legs, something I'm sure she could never do prior to now. I wondered how many times she had been let out of her kennel to run loose. Probably never. But now, she was a black streak, flying across the ground so fast she was just a blur.

Kema was so shy she would rarely approach me. She would cower whenever I would go to pet her and tolerate it, but I don't think she fully trusted me. Then one day she was running around outside and she laid down in the grass in the shade of one of the ten-foot-tall white pine trees. Sneaking up on her so that she wouldn't run off, I quickly plopped down beside her and began petting her on her head, then running my hand across her body and even scratching her.

I stayed there for a long time, almost an hour, with both

of us lying in the grass while I made her feel comfortable and loved. She never attempted to get up.

I think that was our breakthrough moment. From that point on she began to trust me and she didn't run away when I approached her. A few weeks later, she jumped up on the couch beside me and wanted to be petted. I knew from that moment that she actually liked me and I was so darn proud of it. Up until that point, I had wondered if she viewed me as a bad person or someone not to be trusted. I believe a dog can judge a person's character. If a dog doesn't like someone, chances are that person should be trusted neither by man nor beast. I was hurt because I believed that I was a good guy and I love dogs. I would never hurt her.

Her skittish behavior has almost gone away, but she does jump on some occasions to sudden movements. I don't blame her though. So do I.

Chapter Seven: Kema the Swiper

Kema is a swiper.

I rather figured that would be the case when we first got her, since she had no socialization skills and having lived in a kennel all her life. But it was confirmed on the first full day after we got home from Kentucky. We had missed observing Easter since we were exploring caves that day and we had a ham in the refrigerator, so I got out the roasting pan and began cooking it up.

I know the smells must have been intoxicating for Kema, but she stayed her distance because the cooker was too hot to attempt to fulfill her cravings.

After the timer went off and I pulled the ham from the cooker, she was curious about what was going on. Using the electric knife, I cut the ham into several slices, carving around the bone. I had no reason to believe the ham was in any danger, so I was completely taken off guard and shocked when I stepped away from the kitchen counter for a few seconds. When I turned back toward the kitchen, a black flash burst onto the scene, jumped up to land her paws on the counter, and made off with a ham slice. I yelled at her, but it was already too late. The ham dropped from her mouth onto the floor, making it improbable that I was going to eat that slice. Not only did the floor bugs get to it, but anything from that dog's mouth rendered it unsuitable for human consumption.

I didn't want to give it to her right away because that would be saying it was okay to steal the food - like rewarding her for bad behavior. So, I wrapped it up and put it in the refrigerator to give to her later.

Swiping food didn't just affect us, it also affected Buddy. She would swoop in on something Buddy was eating and gobble up what she could steal away from him. There was never any growling or anger from either dog, but the disappointment was evident on Buddy's face. He'd straighten up and look at me with his sad eyes as if to say, "Do you see that? She just stole my food! What are you going to do about it?"

Kema was good about not trying to swipe food for a while, but then one day she swiped about half of a strawberry rhubarb pie off the kitchen counter. Like a light bulb going on in her head, she decided to push the issue. She frequently jumped up and put her paws on the kitchen counter to see what was available. If something was within reach, she'd get it. We lost butter, bread, cookies, and sometimes meat that was being prepared for supper. Once she even took it a step further by eating stir-fry from a frying pan. We had just taken some for supper and some remained. Luckily it wasn't hot, so she didn't get burned, although we were pretty burned up about it.

Curbing such behavior started out by simply yelling "No!" when she was caught in the act. But catching her was the difficult part, especially when Joanna or I needed to be in other parts of the house, doing stuff other than watching her, like going to the bathroom, washing clothes, taking a shower, or whatever. Sitting on the toilet, I would hear the crunch of a plastic cookie package and I would make a hasty dash around the corner to see her on her hind legs, one paw on the cookies, and her head twisted back to look at me. The expression on her face was priceless as if to say, "I found these cookies just sitting here, going to waste. Can I have them?"

We would try to divert her attention and occupy her by giving her a rawhide chew treat, but often she would just end up burying it in the soil of our potted plants. I wasn't sure if she ever planned on digging them up to chew on them later or not. Maybe it was just fun to bury stuff. The top end of her nose was usually caked with dirt and was a telltale sign of what she was up to. When we saw that, Joanna and I would quickly check to see if Kennan was still around or if we had to look for the spot where Kema buried him.

One of the amazing swiping feats happened when we were gone grocery shopping. We had placed a box of Milk-Bone treats on the top shelf of the baker's rack and when we came home, the box was on the floor and the treats were gone.

We were stumped on how she could have gotten them. I concluded she hopped onto the chair by the kitchen table, climbed onto the table, and then jumped across a span of about four feet onto the baker's rack. I was certain there were no places she could have stood on the baker's rack, but her momentum must have been enough for her to grab the box on her way down. However she did it, it was quite a feat.

Yeah, her swiping habits were tiresome. No matter where we hid edible items or made them seemingly unreachable, she would get into something. No matter how disgusted we would get, we were careful not to become too irate because we knew that she was very sensitive and easily frightened. We wanted her to know it was wrong, but that we would never do anything to hurt her, either physically or emotionally.

It was especially taking its toll on Joanna. After a grueling night of Kema constantly asking to go outside and then making crashing noises while trying to get something from the kitchen counter, Joanna asked me to get the crate back up from the basement one morning. I didn't even have to ask what she planned to do with it. I knew. I got it up and quickly gave her a kiss and hug, then left for work, leaving Joanna to do what she felt was necessary. I didn't want to know. I hoped it would work. I could see the tired look in her eyes.

If her begging wasn't bad enough, Kema's eating habits were an irritant, too. Johnny Appleseed would have taken her on as an assistant because she has the habit of grabbing a mouthful of kibble and then walking around the house while crunching on the nuggets. I always thought she did this because she was afraid she might miss something and she wanted to be there when it happened.

While she is chewing, some of the kibbles drop from

either side of her mouth onto the floor. She appears not to notice that this was happening, or else she just does not care. The result is kibble spread on the floor throughout the house, threatening human foot damage. It's not so bad when you can see the kibble, but when anyone walks around at night, such as when we are going to bed and I lock the doors, then there is a good chance of stepping on something left behind by a crazy black and tan "dough-gie."

Chapter Eight: Talking Up a Storm

One of the cutest things Kema does is talk. No, she can't say words like a human, but she has the ability to make a sound that seems like she is talking and she adds head and body language to it. When she talks, she is generally in a rowdy mood or being silly, or she wants something.

When Kema talks, she emits a "roo-roo," and it varies all over the place. Her head tilts from side to side and wavers, as if the head bob thing was part of what she wants to say or maybe she adds emphasis to her message.

It's very amusing and very cute, to say the least. When we see it, which is several times a day, we can't help but crack up laughing. She's very endearing and we certainly can never be upset with anything when we see her talking like that.

We still think the "roo-roo" thing is cute, but sometimes it can be untimely, especially when we'd like to sleep late. I know Joanna also gets the "roo-roo" at least a couple of times a night, often three, along with Kema's nose poked in Joanna's side.

I know because she tells me in the morning, complaining about the awakenings throughout the night, which doesn't seem to bother me because I have learned to tune them out. I would spare Joanna some grief, but Kema never noses me, and, for some reason, my "roo-roo" meter is broken and I don't hear her.

The other time she frequently uses the "roo-roo" is after supper. She's developed a habit -- no, an expectation -- to eat leftovers and lick pans after we finish eating. A problem develops when there aren't enough scraps and pans for her. Unfortunately, now Buddy gets into the act, having learned from Kema.

After supper, we are in the living room, trying to watch television while two crazy dogs are standing in the kitchen, going "Woof, woof" and "roo-roo." If it weren't so irritating, it would be funny.

So, I frequently give in and see what can be sacrificed to the doggies. But I won't just give it to them. I believe a certain amount of work on their parts is necessary. I begin with a simple "sit" which is often moot because they are often already sitting side-by-side, having figured out my training pattern. Next is "shake," from which I get an overly enthusiastic paw from Kema that may scratch me if I am leaning over too close. Buddy gives me his paw as if he is bored with all the stupid requirements. His paw is simply placed lackadaisically in my hand.

The next command is "down" which took a while for Kema is figure out, but she now does it as a matter of routine even before I give the command. Buddy just slowly slumps to the floor.

The latest trick I have taught Kema is "up," which involves her standing on her hind legs to reach the Milk-Bone or Pup-Peroni snack. As for Buddy, it's too difficult for him to go up and down at his age, so I just sneak him a treat without Kema seeing it and allow him to stay prone on the floor. I seriously doubt Buddy could do that trick anyway.

Chapter Nine: Leaving Kema at Home

Whenever we would leave the "dough-gies" at home alone, we always had to wonder if we would come home to a disaster. I know Buddy would never mess with anything, but for Kema it could be a picnic so, during her first few months at our house, we usually put her in her crate. She wouldn't destroy things when we were around, except for an occasional knocking over of a trash can to investigate the innards, and I figured we had to trust her eventually.

As time went on, her destructive behavior got worse, but it only happened when we left the two dogs home alone. Kema would basically make a mess of everything, but she was particularly fond of food. Nothing could be left on the kitchen counter. Bread, butter, cookies or whatever, were stuffed in the microwave for safe storage; but somehow she learned to skillfully attack the baker's rack.

On the top shelf were all sorts of chip bags and, in the top right corner, a box of Milk Bones. There was no way in heck she could get up that high, but she would somehow manage to get some snacks and consume the whole thing.

An empty shredded bag was always left as evidence.

On one occasion, I cleared off the top shelf of all potato chip bags and put them away where she had no access. My mistake was leaving the Milk Bones up there. Of course, she got them, and I wondered how she did it since the shelf was about six feet off the floor. The only plausible theory is that she somehow got onto the kitchen table and jumped the span of about three or four feet to her quarry. I didn't know she was that athletic.

Out of necessity, I discovered the solution to keeping them out of trouble was to keep them busy.

Now, when we leave them home alone, I take a couple of handfuls of doggie treats and throw them about on various parts of the floor. I usually select something like Milk-Bones or other treats that we get in plentiful supply so that it doesn't cost a lot. To make it more of a challenge, I sometimes break the treats in half so that there is double the quantity and double the time it takes to find all of them.

Then I go about the house and distribute them in odd places, making sure they are located in places they can easily access. I don't want doggie treats hidden for years in our house.

My method is similar to using the Kong, which is a rubber hollow object that looks like the Michelin Man. You fill the inside of the Kong with goodies and it takes the dog hours to get it all out, thus occupying the dog and keeping his or her mind off being home alone. I used to have a Kong when I had Thorn, but I lost it a long time ago. My method obviously occupies them for a shorter time and doesn't involve buying a Kong.

Kema and Buddy know the game well and they immediately begin to cruise around the house, quickly snapping up whatever they can. That's when we high-tailed it for the garage and get out of there. Since I have been using this method, nothing has been disturbed when we are gone. Maybe it's just a coincidence that the destruction has stopped, but I'm willing to take the credit.

My one concern is that they might eat too many treats and suddenly have to defecate. For that reason, we make sure they spend plenty of time outside before we leave; we aren't gone too long, and we don't give them too many treats, well, I usually don't plan to. My brain tells me one thing and my heart tells me something else.

Sometimes too many treats are not a good thing.

Chapter Ten: Making Friends with Buddy

When I was thinking about getting another dog, one of my main considerations was how Buddy would react. After all, he had been our only dog for about seven years, soaking up every moment of attention, so I was concerned that he would be jealous of any attention given to the new doggie.

On the other hand, I would often look at Buddy and wonder if he was lonely. Sometimes he would be left at home for hours and, even when we were home, sometimes I would catch him blankly staring ahead. Buddy was a dog living in a human world. Sometimes he would cross the cornfield next to our house to catch a glimpse of the neighbor dog or listen to the barking of a dog a mile away, but he didn't have contact with anyone of his own species. It was natural to wonder if he was lonely for another dog he could relate to.

The whole issue was up in the air, but there was no way of knowing without trying it. He might be really receptive to the idea, or he may not.

His first reaction to Kema, in the crate in the back of the Endeavor, was one of alarm. He didn't care for a strange dog behind him, especially since she was incessantly barking. On high alert, Buddy increased his drooling, which already filled the back seat and flowed onto the floor. I wish there were a market for dog drool because I could become an instant millionaire.

After we got home, it took a little while for the two dogs to become properly acquainted, but they generally had two different approaches to their relationship. Kema saw Buddy as someone to play with and Buddy viewed Kema as someone to mate with. Being able to run circles around Buddy, Kema would jump over the top of Buddy, dance around him, and even subtly nip at Buddy's face in an effort to get him moving. On the other hand, Buddy would always be sniffing at her butt, tail wagging furiously and ears upright. Buddy's behavior became so incessant that it became a real nuisance. We had to do something or he'd be constantly trying to jump on her both outside and inside the house and knocking over things in the process. We made an appointment with the veterinarian to get him neutered.

It appeared that he took the surgery pretty well, not

showing any indications of pain after he got home, although we did have pain pills for him if needed. But the disappointing thing is that he quickly resumed his former activity of bothering Kema. I called the vet about it and the assistant said it takes a while for the hormones to settle down. It would cease in a week or so, she said. And it did.

But the craziness of Kema didn't. Buddy couldn't keep up with her and she would sometimes become overwhelming, so sometimes Buddy would retreat beneath the front steps to get away from her, but that decreased as time went by. While they didn't play together much, mainly because Buddy couldn't keep up with her, they both talked the doggie language and were compatible so I felt reassured that my concern for Buddy being lonely was resolved.

They often shared a couch or even lie on the floor next to each other, so they were completely comfortable with each other, even though they had vastly different personalities. Kema was the crazy, energetic one, while Buddy was mellow. But they did learn from each other and sometimes Buddy would do a dance and bark when he wanted a treat, something he never did before Kema came into our lives.

I worried about jealousy. Kema made no bones about

wanting attention. So we would rough her up a bit in fun and pet her, meanwhile, Buddy would lie on the recliner and watch the whole thing. Pangs of guilt would wash over me, so as soon as I could get away from Kema, I'd go over and give Buddy a few strokes on the head to assure him that I still loved him.

Buddy has the saddest eyes a dog could have. It's difficult to describe, but basically, the skin droops below his eyes, especially when his head is resting on his chin and he looks up at me.

One of our bad habits, before Kema arrived, was to put our dinner plates on the floor after finishing our meal and allowing Buddy to lick them. We didn't have a problem with it since we were confident the dishwasher would sanitize them afterward.

When Kema arrived, Joanna and I wondered if we should continue. After all, we would be corrupting another pooch. Mathematics won out since there are two plates, Joanna's and mine, and two dogs.

Our son, Kennan, had developed a mono-diet, only eating cheese pizza, so he never eats with us. We've been working on correcting this bad dietary habit for years. Now that he's a teenager, we believe our goals are hopeless.

When letting the dogs eat, the only minor detail remaining is how to resolve the "plate drop" procedure. Generally, I finished eating long before Joanna, so I would end up waiting for her to finish, which sometimes took decades before we could put our plates on the floor at the same time. She's a slow eater. Anytime I'd put a plate on the floor for one doggie, either the other would look neglected and abused, or rush in to take the plate from the other doggie. As you can guess, Buddy is the one who would look hurt and it was Kema who would take the plate away.

The only way to go is the "synchronized plate drop" – we drop our plates in front of each dog at the same time so that one doesn't feel deprived. Before that happens, I bring my plate over to Joanna and we compare the food on each plate. If one plate has more than the other, some adjustment is necessary, so I move some of the larger amounts to the lesser amount so that they are equal.

"Hey, he got more than me," I would imagine one dog thinking if the food wasn't equal. So far, we haven't any complaints. We must be doing a pretty good job of being fair.

If for some reason I would plop down a single plate for the two of them, I would place it closer to Buddy, hoping he would grab a mouthful before Kema got there. This is because Kema has a tendency to push Buddy out of the way and take over. Then, Buddy usually retreats to sit back and watch in defeat.

In contrast, Kema doesn't beg for attention. She demands it. When I am petting Buddy, she makes a "roo-roo" noise and rushes over to get her head beneath my hand, taking over the receiving of petting and denying Buddy his access. She doesn't like him getting all the attention.

When I get home from work, she's the first one to greet me, with Buddy a close second. I'm not sure she really was the first one all along, or just that she is faster and passes him up, but she likes to get her caresses and verbal greetings first.

Sometimes Kema comes up to me and wants attention when I'm in the living room watching television. When I'm petting her, I look over at Buddy and see his head resting on the edge of the sofa, sad eyes staring at me. It sends a pang of guilt through me as if he feels like he was first in our family, but now we like Kema better. The guilt hangs over me like a dark cloud and those droopy, sad eyes cut through me like a knife. I will get up and go to pet Buddy, with Kema along for the stroll, and give Buddy a few good strokes of assurance and love, from which Kema will try to avert attention. Sometimes I just throw up my hands in frustration at my inability to please everyone and retreat to another part of the house.

Such are the worries of a dog owner.

Chapter Eleven: The Sparkle of Life

Often when I tell someone the tale of Kema, how we got her and how her living conditions were before, the most common response is how lucky our "dough–gie" is – to go from being in a kennel without any attention one day and spoiled in our home the next. Many people commend us for what they interpret as a wonderful act of kindness, especially when it is considered how far out-of-the-way of our normal lives we went to make her life better.

That flatters me and makes me and my family feel good about ourselves. But then I think – we've made out better than Kema.

The happiness that little pooch has brought into our lives can't be expressed in words, nor can it be measured.

Whenever I go to a family function, I know Joanna will talk about Kema. I am certain because I see the photos in her hands are of Kema and thus she wants to share the latest news about her. In fact, I was willing to put money on a bet that Joanna couldn't talk about that doggie without breaking into the broadest grin and laughing out loud.

Joanna's love of Kema is evident every day, but on one occasion I saw how deep it lies. I was in the bedroom and could hear a wild barking and see a flash of black move swiftly from right to left through the window. I knew it was Kema, but something excited her beyond her normal frenzy. Rushing to the window, I could see a black and white patched cat running through the vineyard with Kema zeroing in on her proximity. I moved slightly to gain a line of sight through the window toward the front door. I saw Joanna standing on the top of the steps, elbows resting on the top railing and her chin resting in her hands. The sheer joy on her face said it all. She had the broadest grin on her face I have ever seen while her eyes followed Kema racing toward the cat. If a facial expression could say a thousand words, her face would tell how happy, proud, and amused she was with Kema and that her heart was about to burst with so much love, she could hardly contain it. She didn't even look close to that on our wedding day. It just goes to show you who she likes better.

Kennan thinks the world of her, too. He often piles on her, giving hugs and pets, all the while saying how much he loves her. But the eyes of the neglected follow him, too, and soon he has to go over to Buddy to make up for prejudicial behavior.

We all get a chuckle over her dances in the yard. She has so much energy and she is still getting used to the idea that she can run free and go wherever she wants, although it always has been her choice to stick close to home. When she is outside with Buddy, she wants him to play and Buddy is feeling much older. With that bound-up energy, she jumps back and forth over his back and head, egging him on. Buddy seldom takes the hint but instead retreats to his refuge under the steps when she is in that kind of mood.

When Kema comes into the house, it's like she hasn't seen us in years. Her whole back end swings with her tail, her head and mouth all over our hands in a hysterical fashion, trying to eat up every ounce of attention and licking and grabbing our hands at the same time.

Onto the couch she springs, dancing and clowning around, then plunging her head down into the crack between the seat area and backrest. It looks like she is trying to stand on her head, with her butt in the air, all the while going "roo-roo-roo."

Chapter Twelve: Going for Rides

Buddy never was afraid of going for a ride. But Kema was.

Buddy, right from the start, loved going for rides. Most of my dogs have, but Buddy was insistent upon it. He'd stand at my side when I approached a vehicle and pounce onto the seat as soon as I opened the door. Often, I didn't have a chance to stop him, and if I did, it was by diving and grabbing him as quickly as I could. He would pile into the back seat and make himself comfortable, usually falling asleep practically before we got moving. He loved it.

I often wondered if it was because the previous owner took trips to the Dakotas for pheasant hunting and he just got so used to riding that he fell in love with it.

Kema was the opposite. She hated riding in vehicles. I know she was not used to it, never getting any rides before we came along. When we did place her inside, she wouldn't stay put in the back seat. She'd stand with her front feet on the center console and try her best to crawl into the front seat with us, all the time acting nervous, shaking, and panting. It was difficult to get her to settle down, so it required at least two people in the vehicle – one to handle Kema and the other one to drive.

During the day when I was at work, Joanna and Kennan would take her on short trips and bring along a bag of treats. They figured that a slow, gentle acclimation to riding may help her anxiety, but so far it wasn't noticeably working. Joanna even did this on her own while she was at home and I was at work especially when picking up Kennan from school, about six miles from our house.

Then, like a light switch being flipped, everything changed when I was getting garbage together for my weekly run to the town hall. I would do that every Saturday, without fail, and usually took Buddy with me. However, Buddy hadn't shown the same interest since we got Kema, so often I would go alone.

Kema was taking a particular interest in my garbage gathering abilities, more so than usual this time. The bags of garbage, recyclable plastics, and cardboard were assembled in the garage and I planned to open the back of the Endeavor to place the stuff in the back. This time Kema was ready. I opened the rear hatch and she wasted no time by jumping into the back of the vehicle.

"Well, Kema! I am totally surprised at you," I exclaimed, wondering what had gotten into her. She responded with a wagging of her tail and wiggling of her butt, facing me to get some petting and praise. At that, she quickly turned and piled over the back of the back seat and made herself at home.

"Wow!" I said. "Look at you!" She knew I was talking about her and that I was proud of her accomplishment. Not wanting to be done with her fete, Kema quickly crawled over the seat into the back once again and leaped to the ground. Needing to get the stuff in the back, I opened a side door and coaxed her to it, but she wasn't agreeing to those terms and again jumped into the open back and over the seat.

I figured she was having fun, but I needed to get the garbage and recycling out, so when she jumped out of the vehicle for the second time, I piled the stuff in and closed the hatch.

For some reason, Kema still wasn't done. She jumped

against the closed back hatch and smacked it pretty hard, then fell to the floor. I was there immediately to pick her up and check her for injuries. I felt really bad, seeing her hurt herself like that. But she didn't want any pity. She only wanted to get back in the Endeavor, so I pulled her gently to the open side door and guided her inside, where she quickly took up a sitting position in the back seat.

"You okay, girl?" I asked as I stroked her head. I slammed the door shut and ran to the house and yelled inside for Joanna. She yelled back.

"You have to come along. Kema's in the Endeavor and I need help with her," I said.

Joanna got her shoes on and jumped in the passenger side seat. As we started out, Kema kept trying to get onto her lap, requiring a strong restraint tactic. Joanna needed to keep her occupied and happy.

All the way to the town hall, Joanna was gently bracing Kema so she wouldn't jump into the front with us; but on the way back, I thought of a little trick that might spice up her trip. Most dogs I know, and many I don't know, like to stick their heads out the window and let the air moving past make their eyes bulge out and jowls flutter. So, I opened the window about halfway and watched what happened. She took to it like a fish to water – a bird to the air – a turkey to straw, or whatever. Her head extending outwards and looking forward, she, for the first time ever, experienced the wonderment of dog window riding – something dogs the world over know and love. She struck the classic pose and rode with grace, eyes bulging and lips flopping. The ride ended all too soon for her as we dropped off the garbage and recycles, then returned home.

Riding in a car or SUV was now a delight - something she will never fear again. She looks forward to her next ride and eagerly enters the vehicle every chance she gets. She still doesn't take the journey lying down like Buddy but instead approaches it like a participation sport. When she isn't capturing the wind in her face, she is getting plenty of attention from one of us – whoever isn't driving at the time.

When the next trip to the town hall arrived, the next Saturday, she was ready for it. She saw me gathering bags full of garbage and knew exactly what was up. Buddy joined in, too, this time and both of them stood by the back passenger door of the Endeavor when we went into the garage. I took their hint and opened the door, thereby releasing a flurry of pent-up anticipation. Kema quickly jumped onto the back seat, soon followed by Buddy. I slammed the door shut. They were ready. Unfortunately for them, I was not because I still had to load the garbage into the back end. I was throwing in the bag of garbage, the bag of recyclables, the cardboard, the two empty plastic oil jugs, and whatever else needed to go. The two doggies sat upright in the back seat, heads turned back toward me, watching and wondering when I was going to get the vehicle moving.

Once loaded, I hopped in and took off down the driveway. I braved the journey without Joanna this time, figuring I would have to do it alone sometime. As expected, Kema was between the two front seats, making herself known. As I gently held her back with my arm, she seemed to be enjoying herself. Buddy was too, but he was enjoying himself while lying down.

When I got to the town hall, I unloaded the bags and other items from the back of the SUV and into the recycling dumpster or the giant garbage compactor. An elderly man, Kermit, was in charge of making sure all the recyclables were up to their standards. No placing garbage in the recycling dumpster and no disposing recyclables that they didn't accept. This is where it got tricky.

It might have the triangle of arrows and a number in the

center, indicating it is a recyclable item, but if Kermit said they didn't take it, then it had to go in the garbage compactor. For instance, they didn't take Styrofoam and they didn't take any plastic wrapping.

There was less scrutiny at the garbage compactor. People could throw in just about anything, which only encouraged everyone to throw it away instead of attempting an illegal recycle deposit. The compactor is a monstrous device, with a plunger device on the right end and a huge storage container on the bigger left end. On the door was a handwritten sign, "Please do not go through other people's garbage." I thought that was odd. I can't imagine anyone going through someone else's garbage, especially if it was already in the compactor, but I suppose it does happen, otherwise there would be no need for the sign.

When that compactor first made its appearance several years ago, a key would reside in the switch beside a green button to start the compacting process when the garbage piled up and became full inside the compartment. Later the key was not present, presumably because people could not be trusted with such an important responsibility.

All the while I would be disposing of recycling material and garbage, I would require the two "dough-gies" to remain inside the vehicle

When I looked back at them, I couldn't help but crack up. Kema and Buddy both had their heads out of the half-open window, side-by-side, with the biggest smiles I had ever seen.

I went over to them and praised them, petted them, and hopped back into the driver's seat. All the way home, they rode with their heads out the window, side-by-side, tackling the wind and being the happiest "dough-gies" I know.

Now Kema can't wait to get inside the SUV on Saturday mornings. When we first started making the town hall trips, she would first roam the back seat, often stepping on Buddy, but then place her front feet on the center console with her eyes staring intently at the road ahead. It seems like she believes that was her duty, and it continues to be – keeping a vigilant watch on what is approaching.

Eventually, through the many times we've made the trip, Kema has lightened up a bit and she retreats to the rear seat a little more often. I often open the rear window when we are headed back home so she can stick her head out and flare her nostrils, smelling the variety of animal and plant scents along the countryside. That works great while the weather is warm, but I refuse to open the window during winter, and, somehow, I think she understands that.

Chapter Thirteen: A Step Backwards

I am sure Kema is enjoying a freedom she never had before. After all, she can slide out the front door, take off at full speed and not look back until she has explored her entire surroundings and become exhausted. Then and only then does she turn around and come back to the front door where she is showered with praise and loving attention.

There came a downside to this scenario later the first summer we had her. Up until now, we trusted her outside off the leash and running free. She always wanted to go outside with Buddy and they would leave and return together, so we had trust in her that she would stay within the boundaries of our property.

Her new-found freedom also allowed her to go where she shouldn't go, which included the highway at the bottom of the driveway. That's one thing that I really dreaded – her getting hit by a car. Everywhere else was safe because we had no immediate neighbors and the land around our house was almost like an island because of the hilly terrain. The only way to escape our island was by means of the highway. It's not an extremely busy road – more of a two-lane country road. There are times when no vehicles are going by but, for a dog, you just can't take the risk.

I don't know what provoked her to venture on the highway, but I suspect a new puppy at our neighbors' place, which can be reached by traveling down the highway. Of course, the danger is that cars and trucks might hit her.

One day Joanna was outside. What she was doing at the time, I'm not quite certain but I wondered because she doesn't go outside that much. Anyway, a car came driving up our driveway and a woman emerged to ask if those dogs on the highway were ours.

Yes. Yes, they were. Buddy never goes on the highway by himself, so the probable explanation is that he went along with Kema.

The woman said that she stopped a truck from hitting one of the dogs.

Joanna thanked the woman and then went to retrieve the dogs from the roadway, She pondered what to do. When I came home and heard the whole story, I also pondered what to do.

The only possibility of a solution was to tie Kema whenever she went outside. We didn't want to, but there was no way we could fence the entire area where she roamed and a kennel run would be just a bad reminder of her past. Joanna bought a screw stake with a cable and we started tying her every time she wanted to go out. At first, she fought the restriction, pulling on the cable and chewing on it, but then she got used to it. The only problem is that she would never go poop or pee when she was tied. The problem with that was – you guessed it – she instead would go inside the house and always on the carpet. Our house smelled so bad, I had to make sure all the windows were open and a fan was running at all times, especially when we were sleeping. If the fan wasn't running, I would awaken by gagging.

We went through dozens of carpet shampoo bottles and air fresheners, and yet it still stunk to high heaven. I considered ripping out the carpet, but I didn't know what to replace it with. I thought maybe keeping the windows open and fans blowing would resolve this issue, that the smell would gradually go away. But before that could happen, we needed to make sure she never did it again.

Catching her while peeing was difficult. She would go near the doorway between our bedroom and bathroom while we were watching television in the living room, even after having just been outside, or else she would make her deposits during the night when we were sleeping.

Joanna caught her in the act and scolded her, so we were hoping that would be the end of it. In addition, I loosened the reins a little and allowed her to run free, especially at night. She didn't go too far after dusk because of all the coyotes howling all around us.

Anyway, it seemed to work. She didn't defecate or pee in the house again. We're cautiously waiting for that moment to return, but so far - so good.

Chapter Fourteen: A Dog's Tail

Kema didn't have a very kind beginning in her life. She spent the majority of it in a kennel, devoid of human interaction, the ability to run free, and the most important element of all: love.

With us, she is determined to make up for lost time. If Joanna or I am sitting on the couch, Kema spies her opportunity and hops up beside me or her and begins her demand for petting. Because she is so damn cute, she gets petted right away and she eats it up. Petting can go on for a long time – 15 or 20 minutes – and we get tired of doing repetitive things for that long, but Kema doesn't, so whenever we quit, a front paw is quickly put forward, landing on an arm or anything available with a pleading look.

"Keep it up," Kema seems to say. "Why did you quit?" I take quite a bit of abuse from those paws, which she uses like humans use hands. I have seen her grasp things with her paws, especially food from the kitchen counter. And when she stands on her hind legs, she is one of the best boxers I have ever seen, giving me a one-two punch.

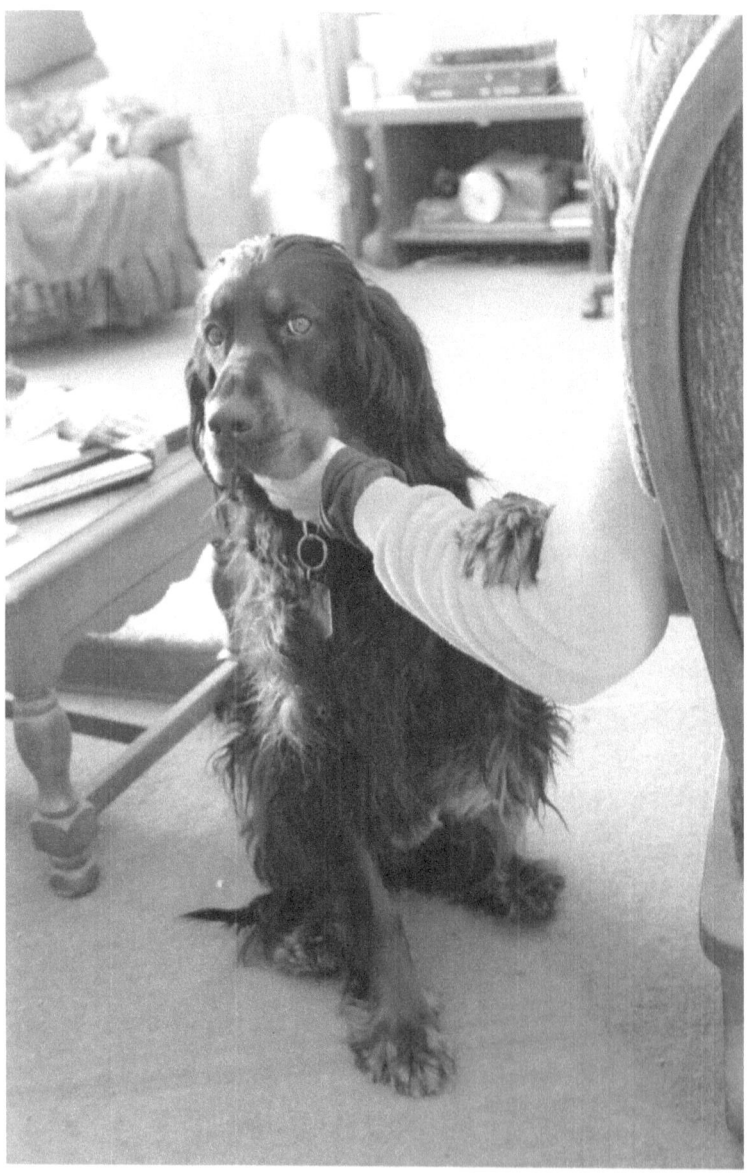

"Thunk, thunk, thunk," the noise emanates as she walks, her tail whapping against the wall or whatever. We know her tail can injure, maim, or kill, so we avoid it at all costs whenever we see it swinging wildly.

When I saw Kema for the first time in her kennel in Kentucky, I was concerned about her tail. The last six or so inches of it was devoid of any hair and the skin was dry and cracked. I was thinking that maybe the hair was so badly tangled and soiled, that maybe it was trimmed off. I knew that Alice had taken her to the groomer prior to my arrival.

"Will it grow back?" I asked her.

"Oh yes," she replied with no specifics as to what happened. So, I took her word for it. Yes, some hair has grown back and, for the most part, covers the skin sort of like a bald man's comb-over. You really can't tell upon casual observation, but if you look closely, you can see the exposed skin on her tail. It never grew back on the damaged area. No biggie, I guess. I still love her just the same.

It was rather terrifying one night when I arrived home and parked in the shed, which I had been doing instead of parking inside the garage because I had a mechanical project occupying the garage at the time. I walked into the darkness and heard a loud "boom, boom, boom" coming from inside the metal shed. I thought maybe something had just fallen over, although I couldn't imagine what it could be. I paused for a few seconds, then rounded the front of the shed and moved towards the house. Along the outer edge of the shed appeared Kema, walking up to get her petting as I usually do.

Then I finally realized what the loud noise was. It was Kema walking along the edge of the shed, banging her tail in excitement against the metal sides. She gets excited whenever a family member comes home.

I believe that dogs' tails are good representations of who they are. You can instantly tell what their emotional state is and what they are thinking, just by looking at their tail.

A dog's tail is an extension of who they are.

Not only does it offer a way to gauge their mental state, but it is also a thing of great beauty and pride. Dogs love their tails, just as young girls love their long hair. When a dog's tail is high in the air, the dog feels proud and majestic. A dog who shows off his or her tail is like walking down a runway during a beauty pageant, or a man's flexing of muscles during a body-building contest. A dog without his or her tail is a dog who has lost some of his or her identity. How sad. Every dog needs a tail.

For that reason, and many more, I don't understand why people have their dogs' tails cut off or, more politely put, "docked."

Sure, certain breeds are held to certain standards, such as Doberman pinschers, Springer spaniels, and the like, and they probably would be judged adversely in a dog show if their tails weren't docked. Maybe those standards need to be reexamined. But if a dog is a pet, which they all should be regardless of other duties, they should be allowed to keep their tails. It's a matter of pride.

When Kema first came to live with us, her tail was always tucked tightly between her legs and up onto the bottom of her belly. We knew she was not feeling secure and safe in her new surroundings. After all, the only contact she had had with people was bad and she had no idea how she was going to be treated. Whenever she heard an unfamiliar noise or I moved too suddenly, she would jump away, scared.

We noticed, however, the longer she lived with us, and the more we treated her with respect and lots of petting, the more her tail would come out from beneath and show itself.

When Kema began to show some of her spunk and exuberance, her tail was out to the full extent and high into the air. She would strut around the yard in a full dominant pose, barking and announcing to the world that this was her turf and she was in control. Joanna and I would laugh and puff out our chests, being the proud parents of a spitfire doggie who melts our hearts every time she looks at us.

We often remarked on what a full turnaround has happened since we got her. She started our relationship being a fearful young dog, afraid of her own shadow and having no real place in the world where she was happy. For almost two years, she knew nothing but a wire prison cell, sleeping on a concrete floor among an ocean of turds. Her food was limited and certainly questionable as far as quality, but now she can eat as much as she wants and it is the best quality we can buy. She went from knowing humans as the beings who occasionally fed her, but gave no love, to a life of being constantly loved and showered with praise and caresses. She went from her former surroundings of concrete and wire to a house with carpet, heat, air conditioning, drapes, and furniture – furniture that she was allowed to sleep on.

There isn't a time now when she isn't wearing a smile. And that tail. That tail wags so much and so strongly, that it leaves no doubt in our minds.

She's happy here and she's here to stay. This is her home.

Chapter Fifteen: Getting Fixed

Her second heat cycle since we had her came around the latter part of January and extended into February 2017. It went on so long, I had to dig out an old veterinary medicine book from our bookshelves to see if she had been put on hold or what. We found out that she has the ability to drive us crazy, or more crazy, for 16 days straight.

Sure, the right thing to do was to have her spayed. It was something we planned to do after she had adapted to living with us and we just hadn't pursued it. You know, it's like fixing a leaky roof. When it's raining, you are reminded that it's a problem and has to be repaired, but you can't do it at the time because it is raining and repairs can't be done in the rain. But when the sun comes out and the rain is gone, the leaky roof isn't a problem anymore, so you let it go a little longer.

When Kema came into heat, we had to keep a sharp eye out for stray male dogs outside. Buddy would become extremely interested in her, but essentially nothing was accomplished, which was a great relief.

We are fortunate to live out in the country and far from neighbors, and especially neighbors with intact male dogs. Kema would go outside and roam the grounds, looking for love but, eventually, she would return home unsatisfied. So it continued for an agonizing two weeks, with us never knowing if she was going to come home one evening with puppies in her future.

We know our neighborhood pretty well and I can tell you that none of the dogs nearby are affluent enough to be able to pay puppy support, even if we were able to determine who the father was.

She had already proven to be an unwilling mother, so we always figured letting her have puppies were never an option. It was just a matter of when we would spay her.

That announcement came loud and clear in March 2018. She came into heat and there was no doubt about it. Not only was she driving us crazy, with her tongue hanging out while pacing the house, she also was driving Buddy bonkers. Her alluring charm and bedazzlement were flattering to Buddy at first, but it got old fast. At his age, she was wearing him out.

There was no way of preparing for it. I mean, she didn't

one day tell us in February that she was going to come into estrus in March, giving us fair warning. Instead, it came on like a storm without warning.

What made it more urgent was that two male dogs began circling our house. One was even brave enough to sit on our front steps like he was waiting for his date or something.

I began tying her out on a stake and making sure to watch her when she was outside, but a disaster was just waiting to happen. That disaster happened when I was on my way home from work.

I was rounding the last curve on the highway with the Explorer before getting to our house when I saw Kennan standing at the side of the road. When I drove onto the side road near him, his pants were muddy and he looked out of breath.

"What's going on?" I asked.

He came up to the open passenger window.

"Kema ran away," he said, barely able to speak the words.

"What?"

"Kema knocked Mama over and ran away."

"Oh no!" I said. Looking down the shoulder of the road, I saw Joanna headed my way. "Hop in," I told Kennan, directing him to the back seat. When Joanna got to me, she got in the front seat.

"What happened?" I asked

"I was hooking up Kema on the cable when she knocked me over and took off. We've been looking for her."

"Dang!"

Kennan explained to me that he fell at the bottom of the driveway into some mud, hence his untidy appearance.

"Which way did she go?"

"Toward the bottom of the vineyard," Joanna said.

By then, she could have been anywhere.

We looked down some of the side roads and then I decided to drop Joanna and Kennan off at home. I continued the search on my own. I drove around, not seeing any dogs, and had given up. I was within sight of my driveway when to my left I saw two dogs standing side-by-side near the old abandoned one-room country schoolhouse not far from the end of our vineyard. I backed up and drove down a short distance on a side road, and then went down a trail that had been the access to the schoolhouse decades ago.

There she was, just standing there. The other dog never moved an inch either. I got out of the Explorer and ran toward them. I was surprised that neither dog made a move and I thought I might be able to walk right up to them. Suddenly the other dog, one I recognized as the neighbor's border collie, attempted to take off running. He started squealing and seemed connected to something. I thought maybe the two dogs had become tangled in some fence wire and maybe that was why they couldn't move. The collie began to struggle more, screaming out in pain, and every time he lunged, Kema pulled along with him. She began to cry out as well. I realized that they were still connected from mating and they were locked together. Finally, just as I was upon them, the two broke loose, with the Border collie heading left and Kema heading right.

I called after her, but she wasn't stopping. I ran through the snow after her, puffing all the way. I caught up with her at the house, desperately attempting to catch my breath as if I had run a marathon. I had thought I was in better shape but that run proved otherwise.

When my vision cleared and I resumed a regular breathing pattern, I changed into blue jeans, put on my boots, and headed back to get the Explorer. I knew then that I was too late to prevent an unwanted pregnancy. I knew I should have long ago had that father-daughter talk with her about the birds and bees.

The best-laid plans of mice and men go askew more often than we would like to admit. Now I had to make new plans and I needed to implement them very quickly.

In the morning, I called Kema's vet to inquire about getting her spayed. Sure, they would do it next week if I wanted. They charged $250. That was a little steep for me, but I realized it was probably worth it to get the individual quality care. However, I wanted to try one more place.

Having worked as a volunteer at the Clark County Humane Society, I am good friends with the couple, Chuck and Cheri Wegner, who run the place. I loved that it was a no-kill shelter and everyone involved gives every animal extra attention to socialize, train, and get them ready for adoptions to good homes. In the last few years, they had added a "Fix-A-Pet" service, with a veterinarian performing spays and neuters in the new addition to the building. I called Cheri and she said they were booked up for a month, but if there were a cancellation, maybe I could be in sooner. The cost would be $80. I said, "Yes!" Not only was the price a bargain, I knew I could trust them for the best care.

I called back the next week and found out there was an opening on the next Wednesday. I agreed to the appointment and then tried to convince myself that it was necessary and that she would not be hurt. I also hoped she would not hate me for it.

The night before her dreaded appointment, I bathed her so at least she looked presentable the next day. She didn't care for it, as usual, but perhaps it prepared me mentally for what was to happen the next day.

In the morning, I got up and acted like I was getting ready for work so she wouldn't suspect anything out of the ordinary. Dogs are incredibly perceptive, Kema knew that I was thinking about going somewhere long before I ever made a move to indicate it. I got ready for work, then called her to join me in the Explorer. She eagerly jumped aboard.

Kema never turns down a ride.

We went down the driveway and I turned right, instead of the left turn I would take to the town hall when I would take her along to get rid of garbage on Saturdays. I was watching in the rearview mirror and I swear she looked bewildered. She was probably wondering where we were going since it was not the usual route. A pang of guilt hit me hard. I felt I was betraying her.

She sat upright the whole 50 minutes to the dog shelter, all the while turning her head to see out the windshield and side windows, but never moving much and not making any noise. I think she was puzzled why the ride was so long and where we were going. She didn't show impatience, but rather nervousness, yet she still trusted me. The guilt I experienced compounded and was almost overwhelming.

We arrived at the pet shelter and I was shocked to see how many vehicles were in the parking lot. I barely found a spot to put the Explorer and I got out, ready to open the rear door to take Kema out. Another person was getting out of her car when I commented on the number of people there. She advised me to leave my dog in the Explorer while I registered. They didn't want any dog interaction, apparently.

The line was longer than I expected. Actually, I really hadn't expected any line at all. When I asked to have the spay procedure done, I thought maybe five or six animals would get spayed that day. This looked like many more than that. There were about seven people in front of me and about five people behind me. I grew nervous. I started to question the quality of care if dogs and cats were going to be mass sterilized while on a conveyor belt.

"Yikes," I said to the woman behind me. "I'm not sure I like this. I just wonder how they can give individual attention to each animal if the vet has to do so many.

"Yeah, there are a lot here today, but they have two vets doing them, so it won't be so bad," she said. "They really are great." Those comments comforted me somewhat but I still was nervous.

When I got to the front of the line, my paperwork was waiting. I just needed to check the boxes on the things I wanted to be done in addition to the spaying, such as nail clipping, vaccinations, flea and tick treatment, pain medication to take home (for my dog, not me), and a cone of shame to prevent licking (again, the dog, not me). After getting the paperwork done, I went to the next table where a veterinarian told me the procedure, what to expect afterward, and what I should do after we get home.

That was the easy part. The difficult part followed. I walked to the Explorer, brought Kema inside, and turned her over to a young veterinarian assistant. I got choked up while saying goodbye and kissed her on the head. She had no idea what would happen to her next and I felt horrible about it.

I left while I still could make it out the door, resisting the overwhelming temptation to rescue her and take her home. I got in the Explorer and drove away, making sure I didn't look in my rear-view mirror. I drove to work, about 35 minutes away, fighting back the tears.

I was nervous the whole time I was at work, wondering if she was okay. The day seemed to drag on forever. I was anxious to bring her home. At 2:30, Joanna came to my work and we went to go get her.

The soonest we could pick her up was 3:30, the same for everyone who dropped off pets that morning. We got there a few minutes early, so we stood outside and talked to the other people. When the doors finally opened, we gathered inside while a woman with a stack of paperwork walked through a back door and sat at one of the counters.

"I'm going to take the people with dogs first," she said. I looked at the other people and nobody was moving.

"Do you have a dog?" I asked all of them in general, afraid to go first because that might be considered rude to the people who had arrived before us. Each of them said they had cats, so I went up to the counter. Meanwhile, an assistant went to the back to get Kema.

I was paying and taking care of details when Kema came through the doorway and to Joanna. She was keeping her head low and sniffing around the room. She acknowledged my petting her head, but I knew it was time to get out of there. I lifted her into the Explorer and Joanna sat in the back seat with her all the way home.

Once in the garage, I carried her into the house and placed her on our bed. I figured she was most comfortable there and she stayed there, dropping off to sleep and waking up once in a while, all the time being petted and pampered.

I thought she might respond to some snacks, even meat, but no go. She wouldn't eat anything. I needed to get a pain pill in her and I couldn't even get her to swallow it by disguising it in a piece of cheese. Worse yet, she wouldn't drink. I became concerned. Her eyes were sad and held no shine.

I figured I would take her to the vet in the morning if she wasn't better. I needed to get a pain pill in her, so I placed it in the back of her mouth and gently pushed it with my forefinger into her throat until she swallowed.

Since she was taking up my entire side of the bed, I figured it best that I leave her there and find another place to sleep that night. First I tried sleeping on the couch. It was too short for me so my feet sat on top of the armrests, which was incredibly uncomfortable. Then I got an air mattress up from the basement and tried sleeping on the floor. I slept for a short time and woke up in pain. My body hurt so bad, I retreated to the recliner. By that time the aches throbbed so I got no sleep at all.

In desperation, I looked at the bed to see how Kema was lying. She was up by my pillow, stretched down toward the end of the bed, just like a human. But there was enough room at the end of the bed if I were to lie crosswise on it. I did that and I suddenly realized that Kema and I had switched our regular positions on the bed but now she had the best spot. She suddenly was the Alpha dog and I had been reduced to the Beta dog ranking.

I didn't get to sleep before Joanna woke up. She insisted I take her spot. She said she'd sleep on the couch, which was the perfect size for her since she is much shorter. I was reluctant to allow her to suffer instead of me, but I was so darn tired, I would have done anything for a little shuteye.

I slept very well the rest of the night and, in the morning, found that Kema had hardly moved from her spot. After considerable petting and begging, she still wouldn't move and certainly not off the bed. I decided that she needed to move. After all, when humans have surgery in the hospital, they try to get them up and moving as soon as possible.

I picked her up, despite her slight objection, carried her to the living room, and lightly deposited her on her feet in the middle of the floor. I noticed her eyes were shiny and bright, her stance much better and her attitude slightly better. I brought her a bowl of water and she refused any, so I knew she wasn't completely recovered. She wouldn't take any food, not even cheese, so as much as I hated to, I forced another pain pill down the back of her mouth. I went to work but was determined to call home to check on her condition.

About noon, I called home to find that she had gone outside and peed, came back in and drank and ate. She was much better and getting around fine. I was much relieved.

I came home that day to find a completely different dog. She wasn't back to her crazy self, but she was at least halfway there, running around, eating, drinking, and jumping up on the bed.

She got better each day. I'm glad we had her spayed. The

time of her surgery and after was really scary; but now that it's done, we have the assurance that we won't go through the fear that she might get pregnant and we won't have to go through that behavior when she's in heat that drives us all insane.

Chapter Sixteen: Snow

I was waiting with anticipation to see how Kema would react to snow. I was pretty sure she had never seen snow before since it doesn't fall too often in Kentucky. So when the first significant snowfall happened in November, I eagerly waited by the window as Joanna let her out the door.

It was a kind of "stop and look at this stuff on the ground and gaze up into the sky at the falling flakes" moment. But that didn't last too long and she ran as fast as she could across the backyard and through the fluffy stuff. Soon her nose dove beneath the surface and came out with a white coating on her head.

She loved it.

I knew that my previous Gordon, Thorn, did as well, but I wasn't sure if it was a Gordon or an individual thing. Judging from what I have seen and what I have heard from other Gordon setter owners, I have concluded one thing: Gordon setters were made for snow.

Ever since that first encounter with snow, she is eager to get back into it. Whenever we go on walks, she is busy running through the stuff and burying her head beneath, perhaps checking for mice that live below the surface.

While we were walking around the vineyard, she suddenly became very interested in one area along a row of vines. She was being very stealthy, standing still and listening to something. Then, all of a sudden, Kema plunged her nose beneath the surface of the snow and promptly brought up a shrew in her mouth.

When she spit it out onto the snow surface, it was dead, and she looked at me very proudly. She got plenty of praise from me, even though I really didn't need a shrew at the moment, because she had accomplished something extraordinary and she was really proud of herself. I was too, like a proud poppa.

Similarly, one of the times that she went outside and came back in, which happens about 50 million times a day, she appeared at the door with something in her mouth right after the first snowfall. I couldn't quite make out what it was, but I intended to find out. As I opened the door a crack, I reached down to intercept as she came in. But she was wary of that move and streaked by me in a flash. Going to the center of the living room floor, she promptly sat, so upright and dignified, then dropped the object from her mouth onto the floor.

The limp object was a rabbit. A nice big one with its head nearly severed, hanging from just a small section of skin.

"Oh, nice!" I said, staring at the dead animal. But then when I looked at Kema, my heart melted. She was so proud of catching that bunny, there was no way I could be angry.

"Good Kema!" I praised her as I stroked her head. She didn't fight me for it, so I picked it up, put it in a plastic bag, and deposited it in the garage to freeze. Kema followed me the entire time but didn't attempt to take the rabbit from me. Perhaps it was her hunting breeding, retrieving the prey, and then giving it to me so she could keep hunting. I'm not sure, but I know she brought the rabbit to the house for a reason. It was her present to me.

That is just one example of how she thrives in the winter and relishes the snow. Every time we get some new snow, falling from the sky, it's like God is giving a present for Kema. The joy abounds in her and her energy soars.

When she has snow to play in, she runs through it as fast as she can, rolls in it, and dives her nose beneath the surface like a scoop.

The smile on her face is priceless.

Chapter Seventeen: Lost and Found

One of the things all dog owners fear is losing your dog. By losing, I mean the dog takes off and you don't know where he or she is.

When I was a youngster on the farm, we always owned dogs, but we didn't always know their location. Sometimes they would be sleeping in a straw pile, sometimes out in the field hunting mice, and sometimes just walking around the property. My dad always said two dogs were a recipe for trouble, especially two male dogs. They would frequently take off on journeys, what my father called "bumming." We lost a few dogs that way, as did some of our neighbors. They either couldn't find their way home or found greener pastures, so to speak. Sometimes someone who didn't appreciate loose dogs running around shot them.

I guess you could say we weren't very responsible dog owners, but keep in mind the attitude towards dogs has transformed a long way from the 1960s. Back then, they were viewed as animals, which they are, but their status isn't what it is today. I remember my mother would not allow a dog in the house under any conditions. Houses were for humans, not animals, she would say. She eventually softened and allowed me to bring an Irish setter into the house, first for a few minutes during a day and then permanently.

We never considered neutering or spaying our dogs. I don't think it was as common as it is today, but I know I had never heard of it in my early years. In hindsight, it might have prevented our dogs from "bumming" and risking injury or loss.

When I became an adult (as a side note, my wife still isn't sure if I ever made that progression into adulthood), I would acquire a puppy, or often an adult dog, and wanted to make sure he or she would know the boundaries of my property and not to go beyond those boundaries. So, for the first few months, I never let the dog off the leash or tie-out stake and cable. I would take the dog on frequent walks around the boundaries of our four acres and never beyond, hoping to instill a sense of what our home territory is and what is not. Some peeing by me around the perimeter also seemed to help, or so I like to think. My scent-marking the outer perimeter may have set the outer boundaries, but I guess I'll never know if my theory is correct.

When we got Kema, I would take frequent walks, both day and night, with Kema pulling me along on the leash. I was afraid that if I let her run loose right away, she might run and keep on running until she ended up in Minnesota or somewhere.

She knew nothing about "heeling," as in walking beside someone, but she didn't need a lecture on how to behave at that point. She was already traumatized by the sudden shift in living conditions, now living in a house with people instead of being locked up in a kennel all by herself.

"One thing at a time," I figured. She could learn obedience commands later, maybe once we bonded, she trusted us, and she wanted to obey our commands because she loved us.

The perimeter training went well and after a month or so of supervised snooping and sniffing and urinating, I thought it might be time to take a chance. She trusted us, came when we called and, in general, she was happy with her new home.

"There you go, Kema," I said as I squatted beside her,

unsnapping the leash from her collar. "Now stick around. Don't go too far."

She set off, tail high in the air. I watched as she ran around like she couldn't believe her great fortune. She ran like the wind, but always turning back toward me before reaching the edge of the boundaries I taught her.

Maybe it was her hunting instinct that kept her nearby, the bred-in process that told her to stay within sight of her master. Or maybe it was just her wanting to be around us and stay within her territory. Whatever the reason, it seems like we didn't have to worry too much. She wouldn't even go to the other side of our vineyard unless one of us was with her.

There was still the danger of the highway at the bottom of our driveway. I made extra emphasis on our walks that she never go on, or even near, the road. When I would go to get the mail, the mailbox was across the highway, so I would have her sit, if possible, and wait for me to return. When she wouldn't be patient enough to sit for that long, I would walk backward, saying "Stay," while holding out my palm to her. If she crept toward me, I'd correct her by stopping and saying, "No!"

We often watched her run loose from the windows in our house and it seemed like we had a very obedient and loving dog, one that we didn't need to worry about running too far.

To this day, when she wants to go outside, whether it's to go poop or pee or just to see if there are rabbits outside to chase, she goes to the door and makes sure she gets our attention. Buddy usually goes with her. When one of them wants back in, either Buddy or Kema jumps against the door so that we hear a "boom" inside.

In the coming months, we split our sides laughing at her antics. It was as if she had never been allowed to run free before, and I believe she hadn't because she would jump over Buddy, twirl, spin around like a top, then take off in any direction. I recorded several videos of her hilarious maneuvers and still crack up whenever I view them. She never left our property and I was quite proud of her.

We were never really worried too much about her not coming back from her snooping adventures, that is, until that one summer night when rain was imminent.

We knew rain was on the way. We could feel it in the air and see the dark clouds in the west. An occasional rumble of thunder gave us a hint that something was about to happen.

The dogs wanted to go outside and I figured if they need to go pee, they had better do it then. Once it started raining, there was no way of knowing how long it might last.

The sky had really gotten dark and sprinkles had begun to fall when I heard a "boom" on the door. Good, I thought, the dogs would be inside before the rain began to fall. I opened the door to see Buddy standing there, but only Buddy.

I let him in and then began to call outside for Kema. I wanted her inside before she became a drenched doggie. I called and called, but there was no response. No happy, tail-wagging black-and-tan little girl running my way. I got a little more desperate and went completely outside, cupping my hands to my mouth and yelling for her in every direction. No Kema.

I went back inside to retrieve Joanna and Kennan, and we all shouted and walked around the property in earnest, trying to find our precious puppy. Although she was no longer a puppy, we still call her one as a term of endearment.

As I ran around our property, the thunder grew closer

and closer, bringing with it a sense of urgency that I had a definite deadline for finding her. The dark clouds were looming overhead, ready to release their load of raindrops. Three voices rose above the rumblings, all shouting the same name, "Kema! Kema!"

The rain began to fall and, in a sense of defeat, we all retreated to inside the house. I was not ready to give up, so I climbed aboard the Explorer and set out to drive the nearby roads for any sight of a young black and tan dog. The rain obscured my vision as it came down in buckets, but I tried my best. When I had covered every nearby road where I thought I might possibly find Kema, I returned home defeated and dejected. I drove into the garage, then walked inside the house.

There was Kema.

"Where did you find her?" I asked, happy and curious.

"You will never guess where," Joanna said.

"Where?"

"In the basement."

"What? How can that be? I know I let her out the front door."

"She must have jumped through the basement window."

Then it all made sense. I had left the two windows open that day to air out the basement. Neither had screens on them because the windows didn't come with any and I was too lazy to ever check into buying any from the hardware store.

Kema had jumped in to avoid the thunder and rain, and the stairs door had prevented her from getting upstairs.

"Well, thank God she is safe," I said, kneeling to hug and kiss her.

Chapter Eighteen: Competition or Friends

The relationship between Kema and Buddy is difficult to define. I do think they love each other, but I don't think it would be a type of love as a husband and wife or boyfriend and girlfriend.

It's maybe like love from within the family, like brother and sister, but maybe a little more than that.

I've seen Kema licking Buddy's ear or his mouth. Sometimes they will sleep on the couch together, with Kema's head resting on Buddy's back.

I know that most of the time when one dog has to go outside, the other one must also go along.

To evaluate their relationship in human terms is nearly impossible. Dogs do not fall in love, get married, and then have children. However, I do think they have a strong bond that would be severely disrupted to their mental states if one of them were not around.

One dog feeds off the other, such as barking at

something outside, begging for food, or just any crazy dancing and barking behavior. One starts it and the other one usually follows suit.

Outside, their habits are totally different. They seem to go their own separate ways, although they are doing the same thing: smelling what animal recently crossed their territory. While Buddy tends to stay in the open areas, such as on mowed grass, down the driveway, and around the buildings, Kema likes rugged adventure. She goes through the weeds and tall grasses to seek out the unsuspecting bird or other creature hiding within.

It seems like Buddy prefers not to get wet or dirty, and Kema prefers to get wet and dirty. That's why we have a towel right inside the door.

However, there are times when they interact outside. It's usually Kema interacting with Buddy and Buddy wanting her to stop it. There are times when Kema has so much pent-up energy and she can't contain it any longer. She'll do spins and jumps and sudden runs in any direction. It's those times when she'll see Buddy and try to get him to chase or play with her. She usually will stick her face in his, maybe nip him a little around the mouth, do a dance around him, maybe jump over his back a few times.

Joanna says Kema is a "bully" because she bothers Buddy, wanting him to play. Buddy will put up with it for a while, then he either attempts to get away from her and go somewhere with limited space, or go to the door and want to get in. He figures he is safe inside.

I don't think Kema is being a bully. I think she wants to play and she doesn't understand age differences. After all, time was something man has defined and animals have no concept of the measuring of time. They know when other dogs may be hurt or may be slow, or other conditions, but I doubt that she has the knowledge that Buddy is old. She doesn't know what "age" or "years" means.

She goes on the basis that she wants to play and either Buddy doesn't want to play or he is physically unable to do so.

One of the most important questions in my head, when I got Kema, was how Buddy would get along with her.

I felt sorry for Buddy, being the only dog in our household at the time and the nearest dog some distance away since we live in the country. I thought he was lonely.

Before we got Kema, he would spend a lot of time outdoors, listening to the faraway barks of another dog, occasionally returning a bark of his own. I was sad, thinking that was the only communication he had with his own species.

Bringing in another dog was a gamble. Buddy might like Kema, or he might not. The same goes for Kema liking Buddy. But if a person doesn't try, the world would never know.

Buddy is a really laid-back dog, accepting nearly everyone, so I thought he would be tolerant of Kema, but that was only my best guess.

So, when they first encountered each other in the back of the Endeavor, it was a complete surprise to both of them. Kema was in a dog crate in the back, wondering why she had been placed there and what was going to happen next. Meanwhile, Buddy was wondering why a strange, smelly dog had been placed in his territory.

Buddy's drool was massive – the most slobber known to mankind – because that is his nature when he is stressed.

I held off allowing them to have any physical contact until we got home. I figured the ride would allow them to more slowly understand the presence of the other. Besides, inside a moving vehicle is no place to have dogs get to know each other.

After they were home for a while, I allowed them to look, sniff, and otherwise check each other out. Since it was Buddy's home turf and Kema was the intruder, I worried about Buddy becoming a little edgy about sharing his space. I considered getting Kema her own bowls for water and food, but it turned out they share everything without any problems.

That's the nature of Buddy. He's the easy-going type of dog who rarely gets rattled about anything. In my experience with English setters, that's just the way they are. I doubt it would have worked the other way around, like if we already had a Gordon setter and added an English setter to the family.

Dogs have individual personalities and they're all different, but some personality characteristics are true for nearly every English setter and every Gordon setter. I find that my previous Gordon setter, Thorn, and Kema have some of the same attitudes and personality, while Buddy and my previous English setter, Jam, also are similar.

For people who don't know, there are four breeds of setters: the Irish, the Gordon, the English, and the red and white Irish (which are a little rarer).

I've found that Gordons are much more talkative, bossy, and more independent than English. Gordon setters are the first ones to get in your personal space and cuddle as soon as you sit down. In addition, they're more stubborn and they want things their way.

English setters are the sweet, mellow type that goes about their business without bothering anyone. They also like just about everyone, while Gordons like their family and that's about it. Some people say Gordons are one-person dogs and I know that for a fact with Thorn.

I've heard it said that Gordon setters will protect the family jewels from a burglar while an English setter will politely show the burglar where they are.

The Gordons I have known are nosy. They want to know where is everyone in the family and what they are doing. Kema actually walks around the house until everyone is accounted for, even if someone is on the toilet.

Outside, Buddy walks around and checks out the parameter of the territory on his own, while Kema will do that, too, but will stick with me if I'm outside doing something. If I'm pulling weeds or digging a hole, she's right there, thinking I'm after something, maybe a rabbit or mouse. She'll stick her nose right in the hole while I'm digging.

Joanna gets upset because often Kema follows her around while she is mowing the vineyard. If for some reason, Kema gets in front of the riding lawn mower, she will stand still and refuse to move, obviously not recognizing the danger involved.

That's true when driving up the driveway, too. Kema will walk in front of a moving vehicle, expecting everyone to stop for her.

Maybe it's her youth and inexperience. At least Buddy knows enough to get out of the way. It also could be that Kema thinks she needs to be as close to her humans as possible to fulfill her role as guardian and protector.

English setters I have experienced are often sweet and loving, they're also very sensitive and they remember when they have been scolded. You don't have to tell them twice.

Gordons pay attention, but they will test you later to see if you really meant it. They like to "push the envelope" to see what they can get away with.

If dogs had human-equivalent jobs from which they could choose, I think Gordons would like to be clowns. Nothing gives us a bigger chuckle than to see Kema come in from outside, jump on the couch, then do a head-dive into the cushions. Butt up in the air, she gives a toothy grin and a sideways look that makes everyone burst into laughter.

Kema is very insistent when it comes to getting what she wants. When we hear one of them pounding on the door to get in, she insists on being the first one into the house. Even if Buddy is standing there and Kema behind him, she will squeeze her way past him, often pushing him to one side. I can almost hear Buddy thinking, "Dang young kids these days. Always in a hurry." Buddy is more patient and seems to accept it without getting upset.

When something good has been placed in the food bowl, it's a tossup who will get the majority. Usually, one dog will get there first, with the second one pushing the first out of the way. Both have done it. When we first got Kema, She would take over and push Buddy from food, but now Buddy is equally greedy. I've heard Buddy growl lowly on occasion, but there's never any biting or hostility.

The competition extends to affection, but it's usually Kema who gets jealous. Buddy will cozy up to me to get some petting and, as soon as I begin, Kema flies off the couch, or wherever she happens to be and races to get her head under my hand. It's as if she's saying, "Hey, you can't pet him. It's me you really want to pet.

When it comes to being messy, I think both deserve the recognition of being pigs. They both drag in mud and whatever else from outside to soil the carpet and linoleum. If it's raining, then obviously our walls need watering, or so they think, as they shake and send water flying everywhere. Our walls also are adorned with Buddy's drool, as he always drools with long slobber down to the floor, and then shakes his head.

Kema is not a big drooler like Buddy, but she has her own peculiar habit to match that one. When she drinks, she doesn't lap the water from the surface with her tongue. Instead, she immerses her whole muzzle into the water and guzzles the water. After talking to other Gordon owners, they all agree that is a common trait among the breed.

That would be fine with me if it didn't involve me. If she would just do her drinking and leave the rest of the bowl, we'd all be happy and go about our happy lives. However, after gulping her water, with the ends of her ears having been in the water, she pulls her mouth out and walks away, bringing half the water with her. It is promptly deposited on the floor near the water bowl, with a water trail extending to where one of us is sitting. Then, the rest of the water goes on one of our laps, with her head resting on a leg, seeking affection or maybe approval for her successful water drinking adventure.

I'm sure Buddy and Kema would compete for space on our bed if both were able to get up on it. However, Buddy is now 13 years old and his ability to jump has diminished extensively. Kema jumps on our bed every night when we begin our ritual of feeding the fish, locking the doors, and brushing our teeth. She's the first one to arrive, so she will take up as much room as possible and in the prime areas.

When we come to bed, it usually means getting her to reluctantly crawl aside somewhat so we can at least get a portion of our bodies aboard. She doesn't actually get up to move but crawls slightly like it is a big effort to move and inconvenience.

Once all three of us are aboard, there seems to be a competition for space. None of us is willing to give an inch, so the territorial feud begins.

Joanna and I usually read for about a half-hour before turning out the lights, so we usually allow Kema a little extra room for that time, resulting in our legs being retracted to the point of our knees almost hitting our chins. Once our reading time is over and the lights go out, I usually insist and being able to lie down completely, which involves moving Kema.

Moving Kema is never easy. It can take many different methods and not all are successful. The first one involves politely asking her to move, which is least effective. Sometimes I won't even get an eye open on that attempt. The next method is a more demanding request, tapping the bed cover where I want her to move, which sometimes gets results – sometimes not.

The third and final method is physically moving her to the position that suits us best. That position is her lying across the end of the bed, with more on Joanna's side because she is shorter and her feet don't reach Kema. I need a little extra so that one of my feet can extend to the end of the bed.

When I move her, crawl into bed, and turn out the light, we hear a big "Hmmmmft" coming from Kema. It is her way of showing her disgust with my actions. She's not pleased, I know, but we need to get some sleep, too.

During the night, she may move about and create more competition for space, but generally, we end up with a somewhat agreeable situation.

Thunderstorms are an entirely different matter, however. If we happen to have a thunderstorm in the middle of the night, Kema suddenly appears between Joanna and me. She is shaking with fright and we can't turn her away, so we allow her to sleep between us. That works for a while, but we usually find ourselves on the outer six inches of the mattress while Kema dominates the center. Joanna and I feel like we could fall off and have a collision with the floor at any moment, but we are too afraid to say anything for fear of inconveniencing our baby in any way.

Buddy, on the other hand, is free to sleep on one of the two memory foam dog beds, the couch, the recliner, or anywhere on the floor. The only problems we have with his sleep habits are his flatulence and his running dreams.

Sometimes we awaken to an inability to breathe. That's because there somehow is a toxic smell that makes us choke and gasp for breathable air. Buddy has the tendency to pass gas during the night and it is strong enough to kill a horse. I don't know how many spray cans of Febreze we have gone through, but I talked to Joanna about ordering it by the semi load.

The other nuisance of Buddy's sleep is his tendency for him to run in his sleep. I am sure it is because he is dreaming and I wonder if he is chasing something or something is chasing him. Either way, it results in him thrashing his legs about in an effort for more speed.

His running abilities wouldn't bother me a bit if he did it in silence. The problem I have with it is that he frequently lies against something like Joanna's dresser, so when he runs in a horizontal position, his feet are constantly scratching wood or the metal handles on the bottom drawers. The result is a commotion that wakes us from sleep and sends me into cardiac arrest. It sounds like the world is suddenly coming apart and the whole process has begun in our bedroom.

Our ability to sleep often depends on whether our dogs will allow us to do so. I guess you can say the same for human children, but at least children can remain in their own rooms with their own beds and hog the bed, pass gas, or run at their own leisure and leave us alone to get some rest. With dogs, they have to share those experiences with us.

I guess that's the price we pay for living with the very creatures that love us so much, no matter how much we, in turn, annoy them.

Chapter Nineteen: Vacation

Going on vacation is always a stressful event.

You have to arrange for time off from work, make reservations, plan the trip, organize what clothes and items you plan to take, pack the bags, and if you have pets, find someone to take care of them.

We hadn't taken an actual vacation for years, so when we decided to go forward with some type of excursion, we were in a state of panic. We still lived in the state of Wisconsin, but I'm referring to a different sort of state – the type of state in which our minds exist.

We wanted to take a vacation before Kennan had to go back to school in the fall of 2018, so our last-minute panic began to set in around the middle of August. One of the major hurdles that we needed to consider is what to do with Buddy and Kema.

Buddy had stayed in a local boarding kennel before, so we weren't concerned with him staying there again. When we would drop him off, he never shed any tears. He went willingly – even happily – with whoever was taking him back to his room. I think he enjoyed the stay and meeting so many other dogs.

Our concern was with Kema. Although two years had passed since we had gotten her and she had improved a great amount, she still didn't trust people other than family. She was a nervous wreck when being out in public and new situations. I was talking with a few people about my apprehension of leaving her at the canine lodge and I was advised not to do it, given her background.

"Don't do it. She'll never be the same after that," a co-worker told me. "She'll never trust you again." I'm not sure if this was true or not, but I wasn't willing to take the chance.

Given what Kema had been through for the first two years of her life, I could not allow the possibility of her thinking we had abandoned her.

We decided to drop Buddy off at the lodge and take Kema with us. It would have been nice to take both of them, but we agreed that two dogs on vacation might be more work than we could handle. After all, vacations are supposed to be relaxing, not work, and just taking Kema would be enough work.

Joanna made the hotel reservations in Mackinaw City, Michigan, making sure they allowed dogs to stay, and I made reservations for Buddy at the canine lodge. We packed our suitcases on Monday morning and set off with the backend of the SUV full of suitcases, coolers, and shopping bags full of snacks for the long journey. Kennan and the two dogs occupied the back seat. The dogs like to hog all the room they can, plus move around a lot, so Kennan ended up sitting on the floor for the 20-minute drive.

We dropped off Buddy, then took off across the state for the Upper Peninsula of Michigan. I expected Kema to get all crazy on us once she realized we weren't going for a short ride. I thought she might begin to panic as the drive went on, but that was not the case. She laid down on the back seat and slept most of the way, only taking her out to pee the few times we made a rest stop. However, she didn't pee for the whole trip.

The eight-hour drive came to a quite dramatic conclusion as we crossed the famous Mackinac Bridge. The Mackinac Bridge is a five-mile suspension bridge that connects the upper and lower peninsulas of Michigan and is quite breathtaking. While Joanna and I oohed and aahed, Kennan got a little nervous with all that water around and the height of the bridge above the water. I slowed the SUV down to a crawl so I could take some good pictures, which really freaked Kennan out. There wasn't any traffic at the time, but the idea of being up so high over countless miles of open water and not going anywhere really made him nervous.

Just a couple of miles on the other side of the bridge was our hotel. After checking in and bringing the luggage to our room, we opened the drapes to the patio glass doors and gasped at what we saw. We discovered that the back of our room was the beach and our view was of Lake Huron. A balcony with chairs provided the perfect opportunity for some relaxing evenings.

Kema's ears went up the minute she stepped onto the balcony. I don't think she was interested in the sand or the water. What caught her attention was the multitude of seagulls walking and squawking all over the beach. She wanted to chase them and, if she was lucky, maybe even catch one of them buggers.

I brought along a foam dog bed if she wanted to sleep

on the floor but she was welcome to sleep on a bed with Kennan. She slept with Kennan the first night. The next two nights she spent some time on our bed and some on the dog mattress.

During our vacation stay, Kema went everywhere with us. We didn't think it was right for her to spend any time alone in the hotel room or the car. The first day we walked through downtown Mackinaw City and she was constantly pulling on the leash as if she couldn't wait to check out new places and new smells.

We couldn't believe the number of people who had dogs with them. Seems like we weren't an exception – that a lot of people take their dogs on vacation. Everywhere we went were dogs and Kema would pull fiercely to get to sniff them. We were very cautious about letting her get near because not all dogs were friendly.

There were many dogs at the hotel, too. It seems like not too long ago, no dogs were allowed at any hotel. I guess the hospitality industry realized that dogs usually do no damage and they can gain a whole lot more customers if their dogs could come along.

That is true for us. We probably would not have gone on vacation, consequently spending hundreds of dollars in the process, if we couldn't have brought Kema with us.

One drawback is that we weren't allowed to bring Kema into any restaurants. We usually found a place for take-out food and ate it elsewhere. A few places with outdoor dining did allow dogs.

During our adventures in downtown Mackinaw City, we came across a dog statue, equipped with a hat and a scarf, blocking open a business door. When Kema saw it, she immediately froze, and then slowly crept forward as if in a stalking mode. For all appearances, the dog was real to her. We encouraged her to go forward and we watched as she crept ahead. When she was almost touching noses with the statue, she realized the other dog was not real. At that realization, her posture suddenly relaxed. We had a good laugh at her expense.

Another time she had a similar experience. We walked in front of a shop and suddenly came upon two chainsaw woodcarvings in the shapes of black bears. At first, she was frightened but when Joanna went up and touched them, she eased up to sniff and find that they weren't real.

One area of concern for us is that Kema didn't poop or pee, no matter how much we encouraged her to do so. In the middle of the night, she would want to go outside, so Joanna or I would take her for a walk. The first night, I walked her for miles and she did nothing until we were a few feet from the hotel. She squatted and peed a little, but not much. The second night, Joanna took her for a walk and she peed a lot, but no poop.

On the last day of our vacation, we boarded a ferry to the popular tourist spot on Mackinac Island. The island doesn't allow motorized vehicles, so the only modes of transportation are horses and bicycles. Kema was nervous when boarding the ferry, maybe because the floor was cold shiny metal, or maybe because the whole ship was vibrating from the running engines, or maybe because the place was packed with people.

Kema refused to ascend the stairs, so I picked her up in my arms and carried her up one flight of stairs.

We found a place to sit on the upper deck. Kema hid between the rows of seats and acted really nervous the whole trip.

When we got to the island, it wasn't much better. The streets and shops on the main street were packed with people and it was difficult maneuvering through the crowd. We just wanted to get away from people, so we decided to take a mile walk outside the congested downtown area to a place along the coast named "Arch Rock."

We walked past all the stores, then past some big fancy houses, then past a few resorts and a golf putting course. The sidewalk stopped, so we walked on the highway while avoiding bicyclists zooming past.

We had just passed a small park on our right when we saw a gathering of people at the base of a wooden staircase that extended up the hillside. As we got closer we saw a sign that said "Arch Rock." People were ascending and descending the staircase, which looked steep and shifted directions several times while having a few flat spots as resting stations.

"Two hundred eight steps," one guy said as he came down. At least we knew what we were facing. I was wondering if I was going to have to carry Kema up the stairs as I did on the ferry. I was hoping not because that could get rather exhausting. Luckily Kema took right off and climbed the steps like a champ. Joanna was lagging and we had to wait for her to catch up a few times.

The rock with the giant hole in it was pretty neat. The crowds of people were not so we had our pictures taken with the rock in the background and headed back down the steps. Kema was doing equally well and made it down without a problem. I could tell she was getting thirsty and her tongue was hanging out during our walk back. She tried several times to go into the ditch to seek water, but I kept her away from it. I remembered a bubbler fountain for drinking back at the roadside park.

When we got there, I pushed the fountain button with my knee to make the water flow and filled my cupped hands with water. I did this several times so that Kema could drink from my hands each time. When she had enough, we walked back to town.

We found a restaurant with outside seating that did allow dogs, but they refused to allow Kennan to eat a slice of pizza he brought with him from another eatery. The waiter said that they didn't allow food from a different source.

We moved on and found a stand that sold hamburgers, hot dogs, and drinks, so we got some food and sat under some trees to eat. After I bought some fudge, which is sold everywhere, we bought some small souvenirs and headed back to the ferry docks. We only had to wait 15 minutes for the next ferry to show up to take us back.

This time we rode on the lower level, so no stair climbing was required. The number of people was a small fraction of the trip over, so we sat in comfort and plenty of room, with Kema climbing up on the padded seat to ride beside us.

There were other dogs on the ferry, too, with one woman having three dogs. I was amazed at how many dogs were on vacation with their owners.

On the last night of our vacation, I again took her for a walk for many miles. She didn't pee or poop, which worried me. She hadn't pooped the whole trip.

In the morning, we packed up everything and started the eight-hour drive home. We stopped a few times along the route and Kema finally peed during a stop for some hamburgers. I praised her for the completed task. But still no poop.

The long, tiresome journey was coming to an end when we drove to the canine lodge before heading home. Buddy was happy to see us, but his nature is more subdued than Kema, who jumped all over him and was obviously excited.

The two dogs sat side-by-side for the trip back to our house, tongues hanging out and big smiles on their faces.

We got home and they both raced around the house, both inside and out, often letting out barks of happiness.

After carrying in the suitcases and other items from the Endeavor, I walked down the driveway to get the mail. I expected a lot since I had it held until we got home. To my surprise, Kema came running to join me on the trip down. She was obviously enjoying life to the fullest again and glad to be home.

When I was walking up the driveway, I observed her sniffing an area in the grass, when squatting. I stopped and watched as I saw poop coming out in plentiful amounts. I ran back to the house.

"Guess what!" I exclaimed to Joanna. She shook her head negatively. "Kema pooped!"

It was cause for celebration!

Chapter Twenty: Puppy Mills

Since Kema came from a breeder who looked at raising purebred puppies as a business, I wondered what is the difference between a commercial kennel and what is called a "puppy mill." I also wondered about how prevalent puppy mills are in this country.

Kema's owners were my first contact with a mass dog breeding operation. Not being an expert on the subject, I turned to a friend for some answers on the subject. Chuck Wegner is the director of the Clark County Humane Society and he shed some light on the subject.

"'Puppy mill' is a term that people involved with animal welfare use to describe large-scale commercial dog breeders," Wegner said. "These are places that typically have lots of breeding dogs, don't necessarily pay much attention to pedigree or selective breeding, often-times they are raised for sale to commercial retail outlets, such as pet stores, in more populous areas. Many go to stores in East and West Coast cities.

Mills are notorious for turning out as many puppies as possible for as little expense as possible in order to maximize profit, he said.

"All commercial breeders are not bad per se, but those that are have most certainly tainted the image of the others," Wegner said. "Some states now regulate, inspect and license these operations, Wisconsin being one of them. This has led to better care of many of the dogs while in the facilities. We still regard the required standards of care as minimal at best. Most care provided by animal shelters far exceeds the required standards."

The Clark County Humane Society, a no-kill shelter, has gained a reputation as a "go-to" shelter for accepting rescue dogs from puppy mills.

"We had often been called in to get the pups and dogs out of a mill situation in the past. Now that regulation, inspection, and licensing occur, it is less frequent. It's not that the mills have closed, but some have moved away from Clark County. We have been asked to rescue the remainder of dogs from mills that are closing business in other counties, too."

As for the condition that mill dogs are in, it varies, he said. The shelter workers have seen the terrible neglect of basic medical care, whether it be dental issues, illness, lack of proper sanitation, untreated injuries, and lack of basic grooming.

"In my opinion, the worst condition is the lack of socialization, any kind of interaction or normal dog behavior. This often leaves the dogs behaviorally damaged for the rest of their lives," Wegner said.

"I am in no way saying there should be no breeding of dogs. I love dogs and humans need dogs as companions, working and service animals, too. However, the breeding must be done in such a way as to preserve the bond we have with dogs and must be beneficial to them, not detrimental to their well-being," he said.

"There is a proper way to accomplish this and there are many good, reputable dog breeders out there, but the folks who run puppy mills are not doing it right. Their over-riding motivation is profit and the dogs suffer for it," Wegner said.

Chapter Twenty one: Going Forward

The story of Kema has not ended. It's been two years since we got her and there are many more stories yet to be told. I am certain Kema has many more adventurous years ahead with us.

I often wonder what she is thinking, especially during the quiet times when she is sitting so still while being petted. Looking into those soulful eyes, I can see the love that is welling within her.

I wonder if she still remembers her former life in Kentucky, maybe even in her dreams, and compares it to her life now. I wonder if she appreciates her new life and is grateful that we came all that way to rescue her. Just experiencing the love she shows to us, I know that she does.

I try to imagine the life she had before, being held in a kennel run with a chain-link fence on either side and a hard concrete floor to walk and lie upon. I wonder what kind of food they gave her and how much and if she was frequently hungry.

I also wonder what she thought about, that every day was the same and the highlight of the day is when someone came by to offer her some food or, infrequently, came to clean the floor of feces.

Did she also think about escaping like those dogs that attempted it but were caught and imprisoned in a corn crib? Or was she resigned to the fact that her life would not amount to anything more and that she would never experience love from anyone?

Did she suffer from depression?

The yapping dogs in the kennels next to her were her only companions, who offered her little solace for the mental anguish she endured. Was this the life she would lead until she got to be old, sleeping on the cold, hard concrete floor until every joint hurt and she didn't see the point of living?

I imagine these are the conditions and the thoughts of the doggies that lived there. And because she did live such a downtrodden life, I want to make up for the bad things that happened to her, so I spoil and shower her with love and praise.

She seems to have an insatiable hunger for affection, staying for what seems like hours to be petted. When we stop petting her, she paws us or lays a paw on an arm to signal "keep on petting me."

I often wonder if she is overcompensating for the previous lack of love. According to a friend of mine, Chuck Wegner, who runs the Clark County Humane Society, they often see this type of behavior often in pups and even adult animals. They have been deprived of companionship, whether of people or other animals. It may take a very long time for the dogs to know how to interact normally once removed from the bad situation. In the most severe cases, they may never be able to relate to others in an acceptable manner.

I wonder how long she had been without affection. Sometimes I wonder if she had been taken away from her mother too early, therefore she never knew the kind of love she should have had and never learned how to be a mother herself. Ironically, it is that lack of motherly behavior that freed her from being a puppy mill breeder and set the wheels in motion for her to come into our lives.

Although her need for petting and attention can be tiring at times, it's something I, or Joanna, or Kennan will never deprive her of. As long and she sits there politely and lays her paw on an arm or leg as a symbol to continue petting her, we always will.

I don't believe in being harsh with dogs and I always shower my dogs with praise and affection for doing the right thing. It seems to be working great. More importantly, it is good for me because I wouldn't think much of myself if I was angry with them.

So, in the coming years, she will be given challenges to boost her self-esteem, maybe even taking on agility training.

Since she has food available, I know that she never goes hungry. That fact should add to her feeling of security. She's added a few pounds since she's been with us and I can no longer see her ribs.

Whatever we do down the road, we know that we will do it together – as a family. The life ahead will be a great one because the time we spend together is the most important.

I believe we have gained more from Kema's presence than she has gained from ours. With her love, Kennan has learned to give love openly and unashamed. He frequently tells Kema that he loves her while stroking her head. He will carry these emotions long into his adulthood, having learned to care for another being as much as any human can.

Joanna's life is more fulfilling, having a dog that loves and admires her. Whenever we are with family or friends, Joanna somehow brings up the subject of Kema. She tells the stories of her dog with such enthusiasm that makes her swell with pride. I have never seen a broader smile on her face as when she is telling the tales of Kema and it doesn't take much to start tears of happiness rolling down her face.

I know Buddy is happier with her in our home. His tail is wagging whenever Kema is around. When she begs, so does Buddy. When she goes outside, so does he. While she might irritate him at times, I have never seen him angry with her. They even sleep together at times, with one head resting on the body of the other. I know Buddy enjoys being able to relate to someone of his own species and I believe they have a very close bond.

As for me, I could say all of the things for Kennan and Joanna are true for me also. I have the satisfaction that we have given Kema the happiest life I can possibly give a dog. I know that she is a joy to be around and she makes me laugh with her silly antics.

Most of all, she has brought love into our lives. That is one thing you can never have too much of.

Kema is love.

www.ingramcontent.com/pod-product-compliance
Lightning Source LLC
Chambersburg PA
CBHW030909080526
44589CB00010B/222